CIENCIAS NATURALES 1º ESO
PROYECTO BILINGÜE WORKBOOK ONE

1ª Edición: febrero 2008

Composición de portada: Lulu.com

Maquetación: Francisco José Martínez Ruiz

Editor: Lulu.com

Lulu Enterprises
26-28 Hammersmith Grove
London W6 7BA

www.lulu.com

ISBN: 978-1-8479958-8-9

CIENCIAS NATURALES 1º ESO
PROYECTO BILINGÜE WORKBOOK ONE

María Mercedes Bautista Arnedo
Licenciada en Ciencias Biológicas

Prólogo

La enseñanza bilingüe de las ciencias naturales supone para muchos de los profesores que se inician, un verdadero reto, ya que significa hacer frente a problemas de muy diversa naturaleza en lo concerniente a aspectos metodológicos, de contenido, lengua y búsqueda de materiales. El material didáctico se convierte en un problema para el profesor. Se suele optar por la adaptación del material existente en español o por la incorporación de material en lengua extranjera procedente del país de origen.

Resulta relativamente sencillo encontrar materiales didácticos de ciencias de la naturaleza en inglés. Sin embargo, en la mayoría de los casos, no son apropiados para su uso en la clase, ya que los textos en la lengua original poseen un nivel demasiado elevado para nuestros estudiantes en lengua extranjera. Por esta razón, el profesor necesita trabajar en la adaptación de estos materiales al nivel que tienen los estudiantes del idioma inglés.

Con estos materiales se proporciona al profesorado que imparta enseñanzas bilingües, de un material útil y concreto en inglés, y de una herramienta que permita al profesorado una autoformación para impartir tópicos de ciencias naturales a un nivel lingüístico elemental en inglés, y que además les posibilite guiar al alumnado de forma clara, concisa y fácilmente entendible para el mismo.

Estos materiales están orientados para ser utilizados en un programa bilingüe para introducir contenidos de Ciencias Naturales a nivel de 1º de ESO, dentro del Plan para el Fomento del Plurilingüísmo de la Junta de Andalucía.

En **CIENCIAS NATURALES 1º ESO PROYECTO BILINGÜE WORKBOOK ONE** se recogen actividades para trabajar los contenidos relacionados con el **Bloque "La Tierra en el Universo"** propuestos para la materia de Ciencias de la Naturaleza de 1º de ESO en el Real Decreto 1631/2006, por el que se establecen las enseñanzas mínimas correspondientes a la Educación Secundaria Obligatoria.

María Mercedes Bautista Arnedo

INDICE DE CONTENIDOS

Unit 

1. THE UNIVERSE AND THE SOLAR SYSTEM

ACTIVITIES

1) **Color the Internacional Space Station.**

2) **What's your name? Are you ….?** Name your Shuttle crew for the mission

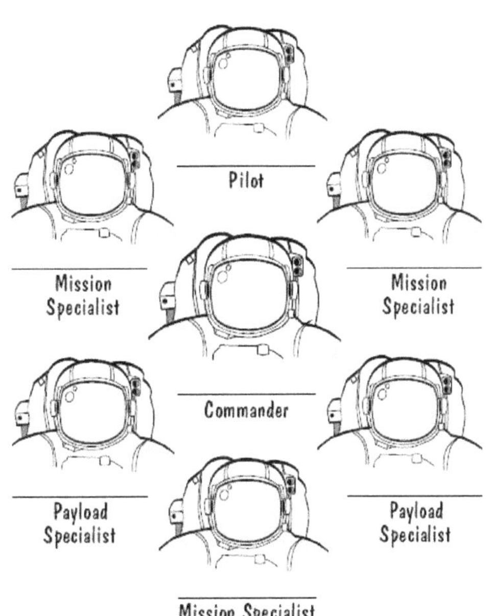

3) **Connect the dots on the Shuttle.**

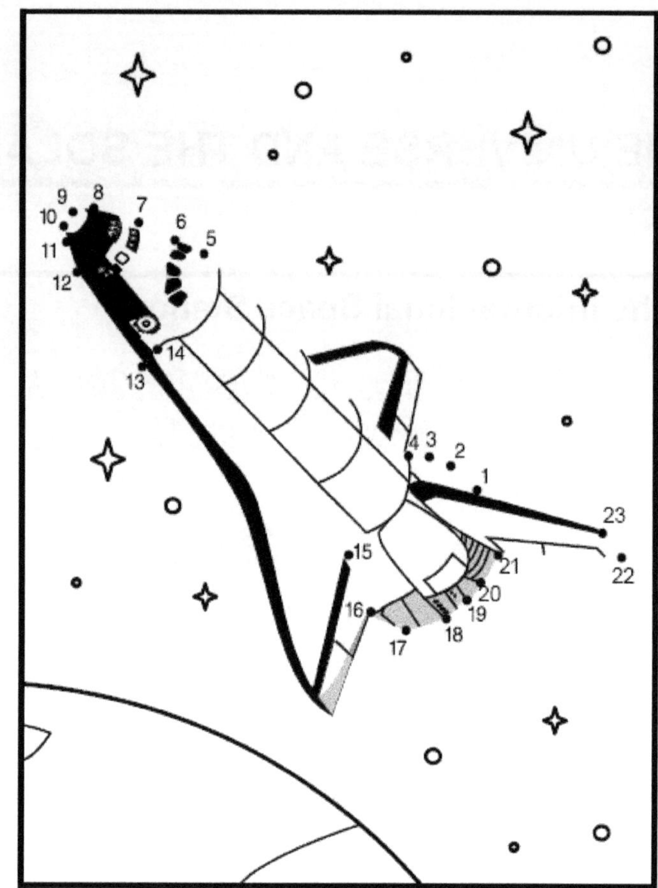

4) **Connect the dots on the International Space Station.**

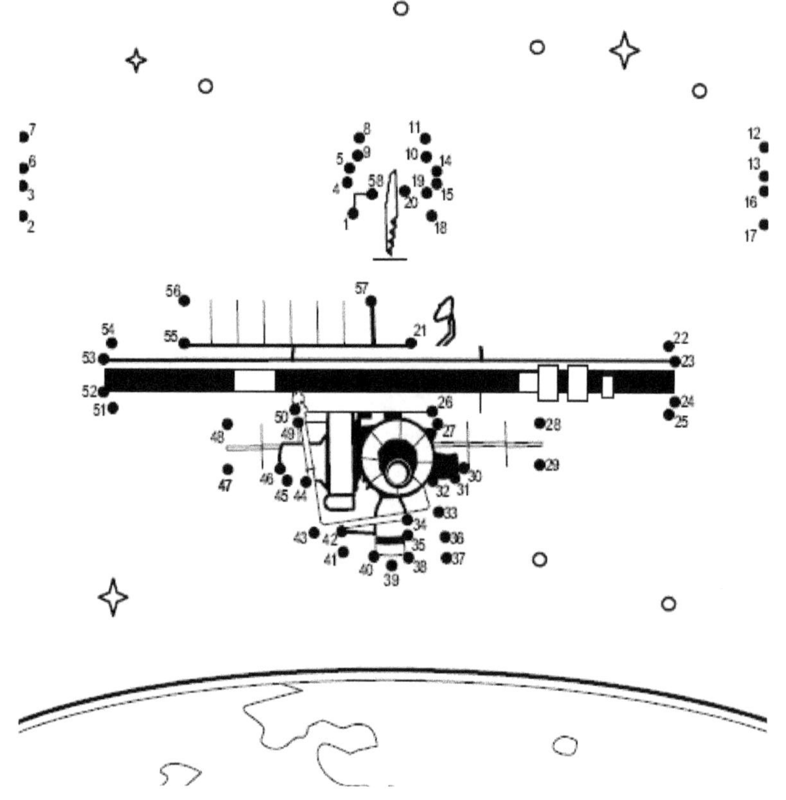

5) **Connect the dots to find the constellation Orion (the hunter).** Orion, also known as "The Hunter," is a constellation in the Northern Hemisphere.

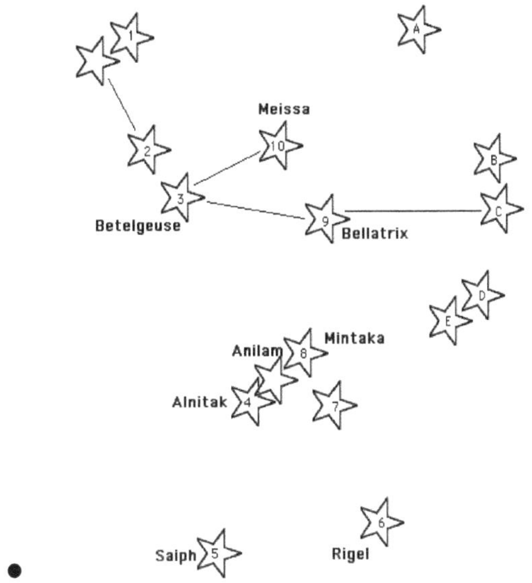

Meissa
Betelgeuse
Bellatrix
Mintaka
Anilam
Alnitak
Saiph
Rigel

6) **Connect the dots to find the "The Great Bear"**

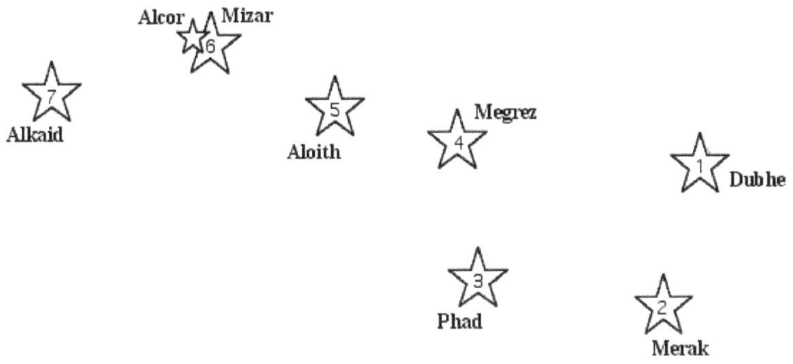

Alcor
Mizar
Alkaid
Aloith
Megrez
Dubhe
Phad
Merak

7) **Connect the dots to find the the "scorpion".**

Scorpius (the scorpion) is a constellation of the zodiac. Connect the dots and see if you can imagine a scorpion. The brightest star in Scorpius is Antares, a red supergiant star.

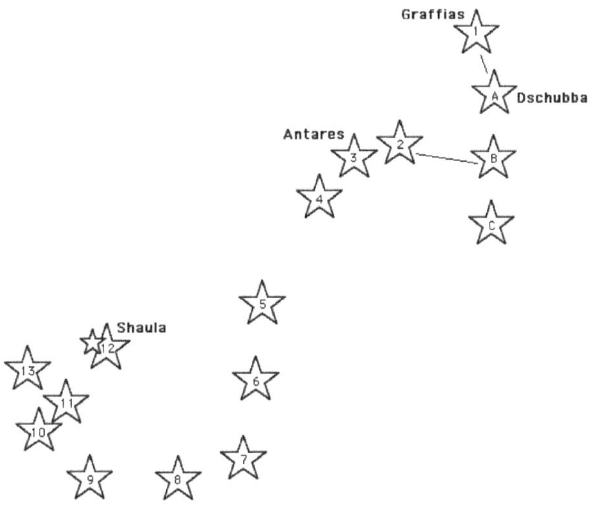

Graffias
Dschubba
Antares
Shaula

8) What do you remenber? Choose the rigth option.

You already know about

- How the Moon orbits the Earth
- All the thing that make up the Solar System

a) The Earth is ...

- o flat
- o an asteroid
- o a planet
- o a star

b) The Moon is ...

- o an asteroid
- o a planet
- o a satellite
- o made of cheese

c) What force keeps us on the Earth?

- o Atmospheric pressure
- o Glue
- o Magnetism
- o Gravity

d) Space is full of ...

- o Air
- o Alien life-forms
- o Gas
- o Nothing

9) Choose the rigth option.

a) Which word means "Sun-centred"?

- o egocentric
- o geocentric
- o heliocentric
- o solarcentric

b) An object which orbit another object is called a...

- o bung
- o moon
- o satellite
- o spacecraft

10) Filling. Orbiting around "TO ORBIT & TO SPIN".

- The planets .... the Sun, the Moon orbits the Earth.
- The Earth ....on its axis.

11) Color the Solar System.

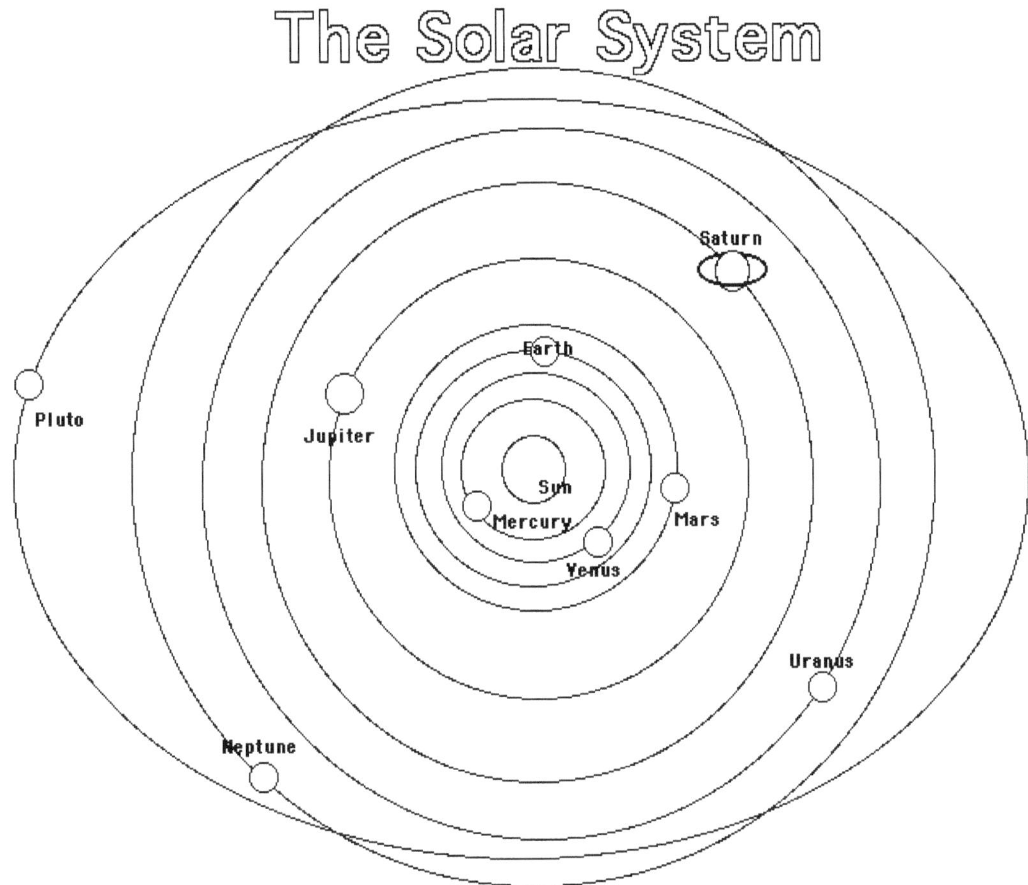

In our **Solar System**, nine planets (Mercury, Venus, Earth, Mars, Jupiter, Saturn, Uranus, Neptune, and Pluto), over 61 moons, many asteroids (mostly in a belt between Mars and Jupiter), comets, meteoroids and other rocks and gas all orbit the Sun.

12) Think about and answer the question.

a) What are the main differences between the Sun and the planets? Tick (☑) the correct answers.

- o The Sun orbits the planets
- o The Sun produces light, but planets do not.
- o Planets move, but stars don not.

b) How many planets are there in the Solar System?

c) What are the two movements the planets make?

d) What are the names of the planets in the Solar System? Make a list of the planets, starting with the planet closest to the Sun.

13) Color the "Asteroid Belt". Read the text slowly and answer.

<<Asteroids are rocky objects that move around the Sun. They are smaller than planets and moons. Most asteroids are located between Mars and Jupiter.>>

The Asteroid Belt

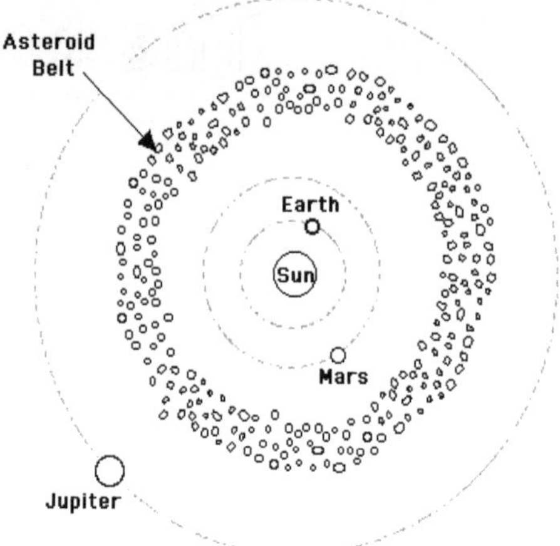

a) What are asteroids?

b) Where are asteroids located in the Solar System?

14) Color the Inner Planets.

The inner planets are those planets that orbit close to the sun. They are: Mercury, Venus, Earth, and Mars. They are relatively small, and are composed mostly of rock. Mercury and Venus have no moons; the Earth has one moon, and Mars has two tiny moons.

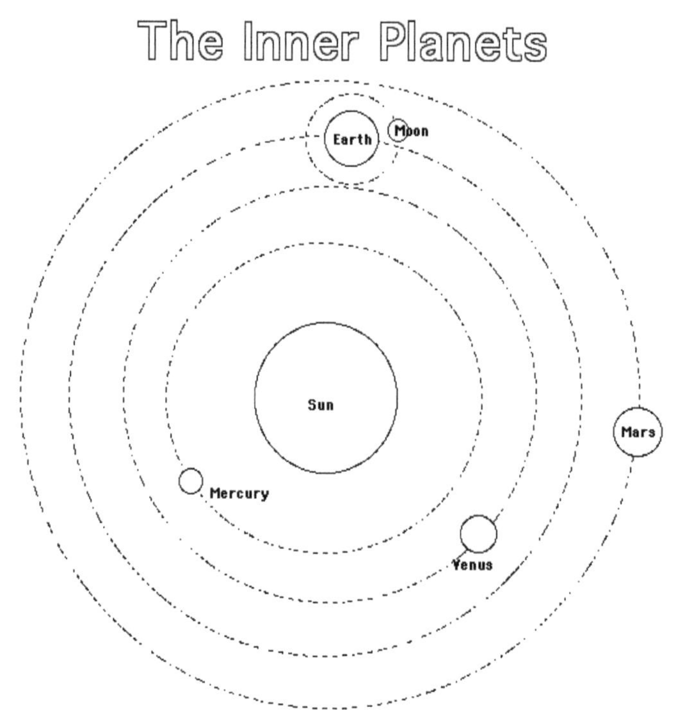

15) Color the Outer Planets.

The outer planets are those planets that orbit far from the Sun. They are: Jupiter, Saturn, Uranus, Neptune, and Pluto. They are mostly huge, mostly gaseous, ringed, and have many moons (the exception is Pluto which is small and rocky, has one moon, and it considered to be a dwarf planet).

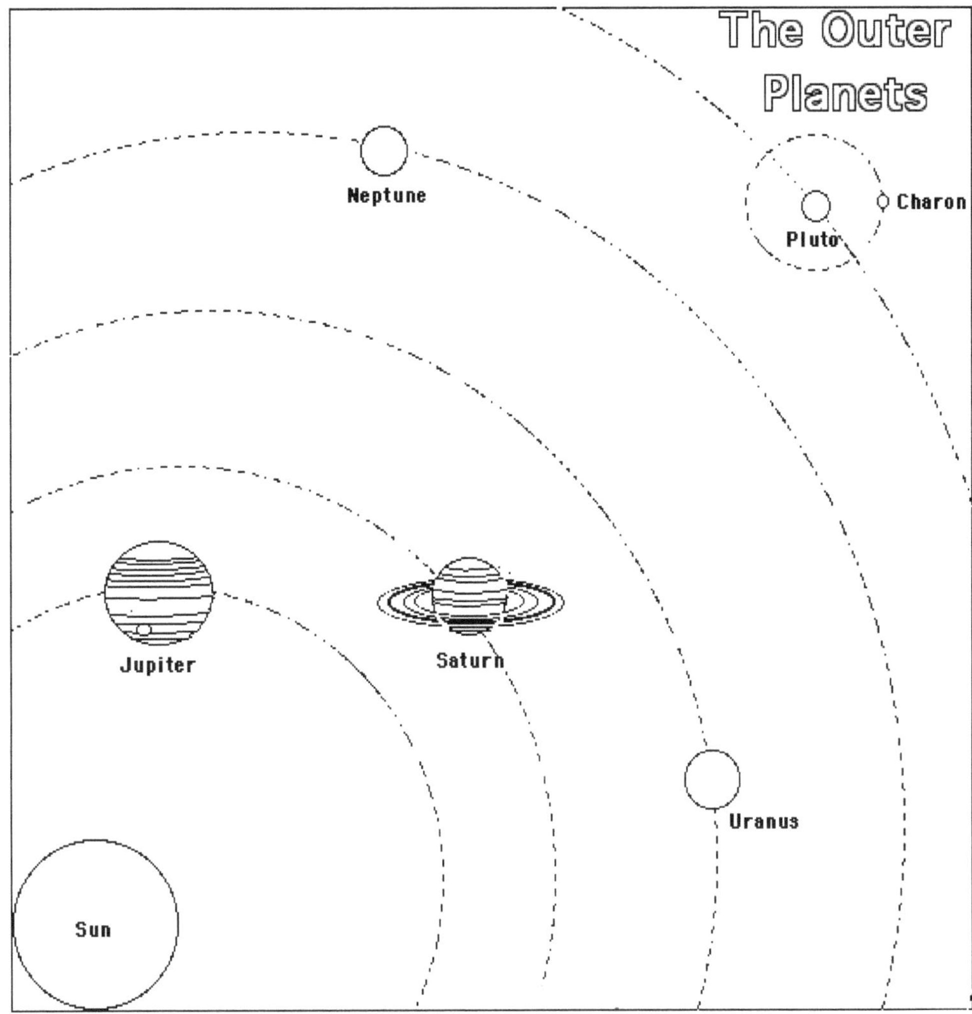

16) Think about and answer.

a) What is at the center of our Solar System?

b) Which planet is the biggest?

c) Which planet is called the "red planet"?

d) What is the name of the group of objects that orbit the Sun between Mars and Jupiter?

e) Are the inner planets made of rock or gas?

17) First, second, third, fourth, fifth ...

a) The Earth is the .... planet from the Sun.

b) Mercury is the .... planet from the Sun.

c) Pluto is the .... planet from the Sun.

d) Mars is the .... planet from the Sun.

e) Jupiter is the .... planet from the Sun.

f) Venus is the .... planet from the Sun.

g) Saturn is the .... planet from the Sun.

h) Neptune is the .... planet from the Sun.

i) Uranus is the .... planet from the Sun.

18) Label the Aphelion-Perihelion.

Label the orbital diagram using the terms below.

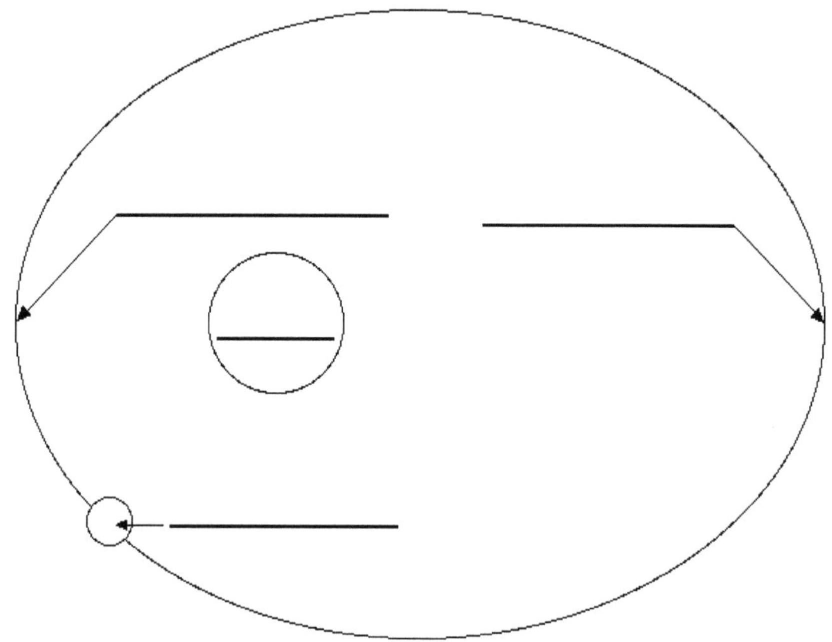

Aphelion - the point in an orbit that is farthest from the sun.

Perihelion - the point in an orbit that is closest to the sun.

Sun - the star in our Solar System.

Planet - a large celestial body that orbits a star.

19) Color the Jupiter planet and answer.

Jupiter is the fifth planet from the Sun. It is a gas giant and the biggest planet in the Solar System. Jupiter has a thick atmosphere, four large moons, and dozens of smaller moons, and a barely-visible ring. The great red spot is an enormous storm.

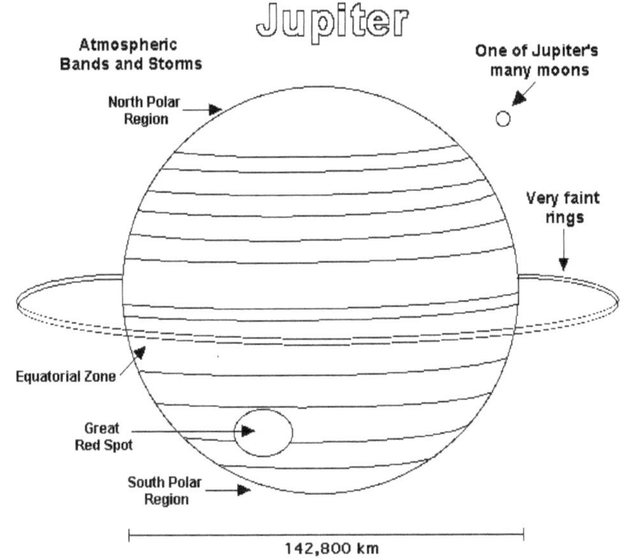

a) Is Jupiter the biggest planet?

b) Does Jupiter have a ring?

c) Is Jupiter's atmosphere thick or thin?

d) What is the red spot?

20) Color the Saturn planet and answer.

Saturn is the sixth planet from the Sun. It is a gas giant and the second – biggest planet in our Solar System. It has beautiful rings that are made mostly of ice (and some rock). Saturn is made of hidrogen and helium gas. It has dozens of moons. Saturn is visible without using a telescope, but a low-power telescope is needed to see its rings.

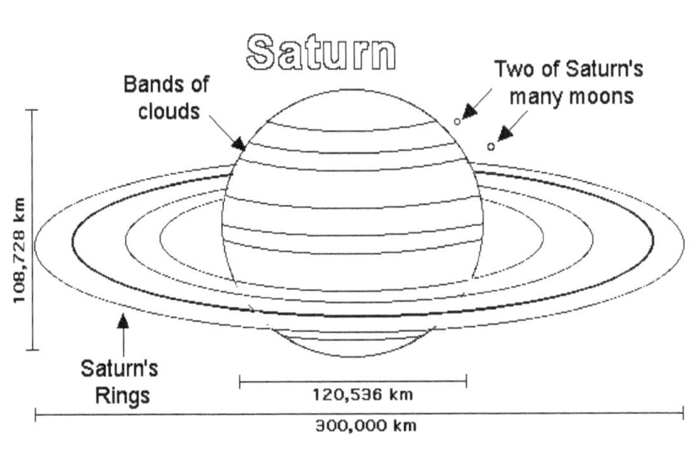

a) Is Saturn rocky or gaseous?

b) Is Saturn the biggest planet?

c) How many moons are there in the Saturn planet?

d) Can you see Saturn's rings using your eyes alone?

21) Space Word Chop.

conste	co	llation	gal
or	ipse	mete	black
orite	eor	zen	gra
vity	met	pla	ith
axy	mo	ecl	hole
net	aste	sate	met
roid	llite	on	bit

22) Space Word Search.

All words are positioned left to right, right to left, and diagonally.

F J C O N S T E L L A T I O N A V X N S J E G

R L P X V B V S C G I O L P Y Q R F E T U X T

K Q D L B Q G L R G K Y U O H Q K Y S O L S U

G B I E A D D A L V H K C I A Q N T P H K U W

K M O Y T N V T M O C U B M O Z K L I J R S Z

V Y P K A I E R U Q A L W C E A G A L A X Y G

Y P Y Z T X A T C N A Z G N A K O T C S D V Q

X P S Y A N P D P C G D I N E Q Y G E L X X Y

G X C K I Y L D K Y T T M R T F N E B H F E A

E Z U K I J D W E H E L P I Z X O W L E T R

D X R Q P V H I M C T D X L L Y R R W Z K I D

H N U H D O J O O E K Q Z E L S J W G S Z R D

W Q S W L E C H O R P G G V E L M J U N K O L

S I E E I N I R G G E N I T T J J E L O E E S

D X W K R W P M T K J T Y Y A W C T W O V T C

E O R B I T J R Y S B S S D S L Q H S M Q E B

W P Z W L V V X K J C C O A V H Z C H U G M B

A O O N A X L R Q H F Q F L E A K F V R Z O P

METEORITE	BLACK HOLE	METEOR	ORBIT
ECLIPSE	CONSTELLATION	GALAXY	MOON
ZENITH	GRAVITY	PLANET	
SATELLITE	ASTEROID	COMET	

23) **Write the name planets in the boxes.**

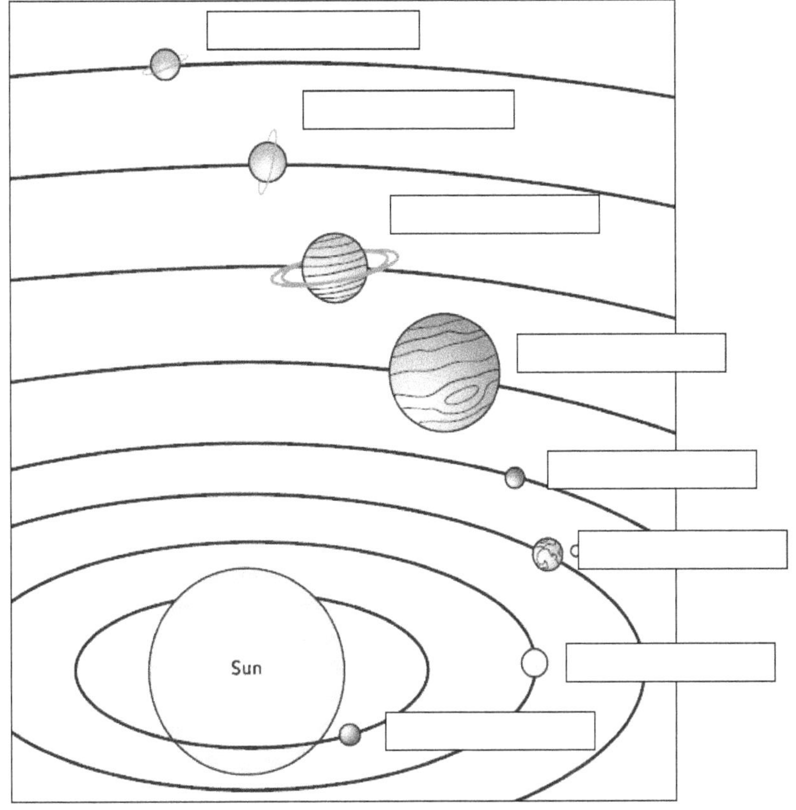

24) **Draw a line from the planet to its name.**

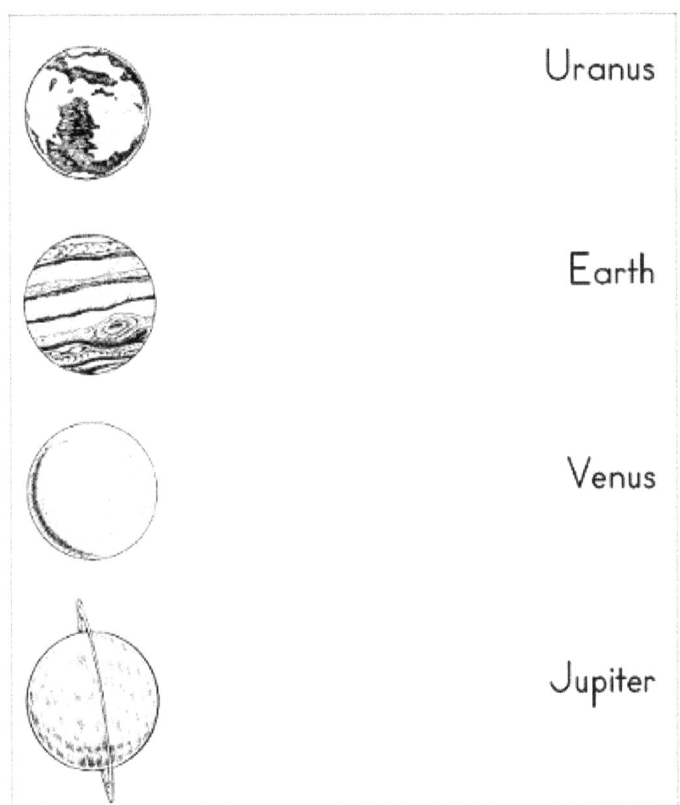

25) The planets are not all the same size.

Look at the planets, and then answer the questions below.

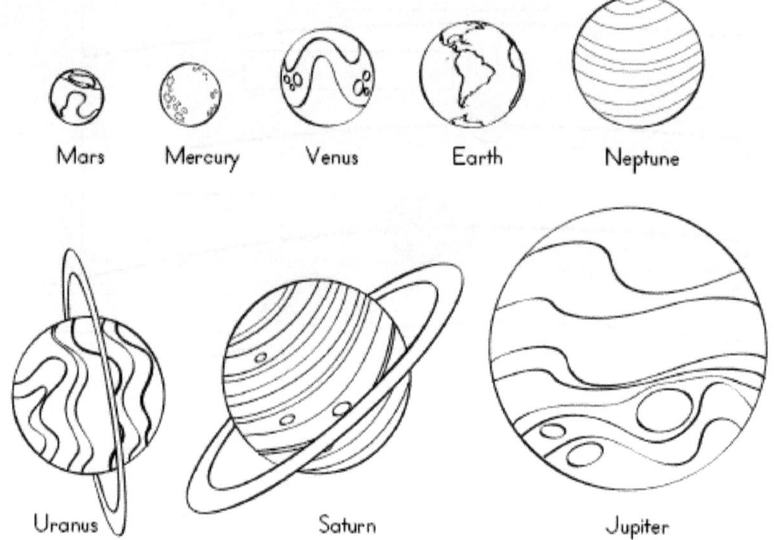

a) Which planet is the smallest?

b) Which planet is the biggest?

c) Is Earth 5th or 6th biggest?

d) Is Uranus bigger than Saturn?

e) Which planet is almost the same size as Earth?

26) Find the words in the puzzle.

27) Solar System Game

http://www.nasa.gov/audience/forkids/games/G_Solar_System_Game.html

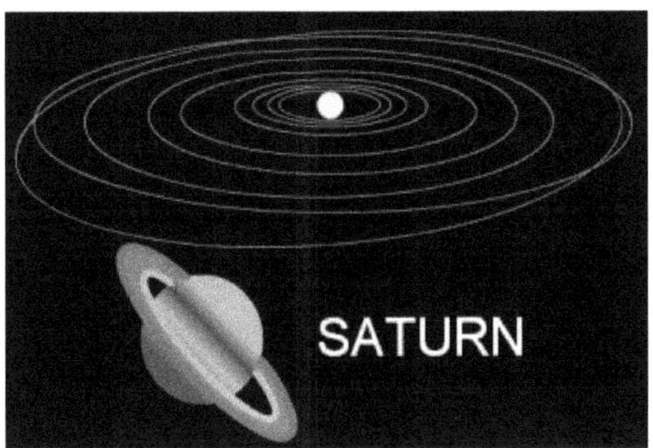

28) Play the Earth System Game

Sort the cards into the correct pile -- living things, air, water or land.

http://www.cotf.edu/ete/modules/k4/online/Eonline1.html

29) How Old are You on Another Planet?

An Earth day is about 24 hours long. An Earth year is about 365 days long. Days and years on other planets are different. Some planets have very long days. Some have very short days. Some have very long years. Some have very short years. Type your birthday below. Click on a planet. You will see how old you would be if you had been born there!

http://www.nasa.gov/audience/forkids/games/age.html

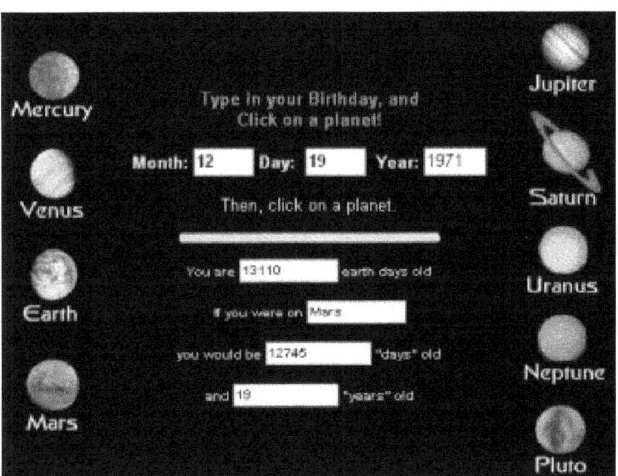

30) Connect the Stars!

Play connect the dots with the constellations!

http://www.nasa.gov/audience/forkids/games/connect.html

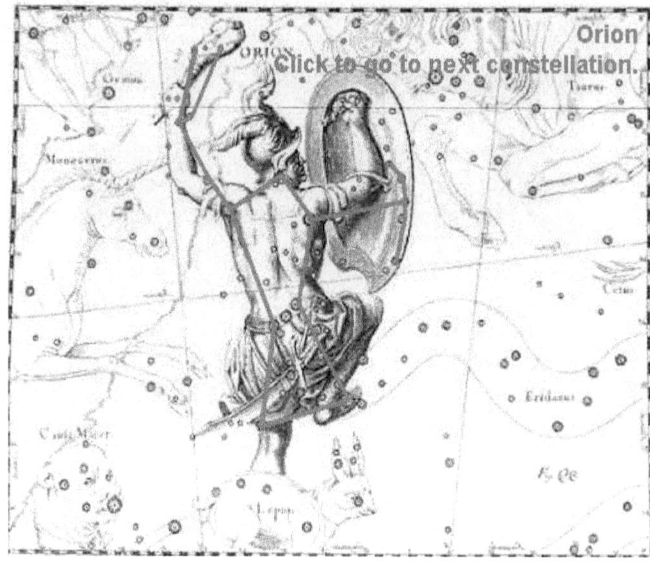

31) Solar System Trading Cards

Print out onto card stock or heavy paper. Cut out and fold in half along dotted line; glue or tape each card together.

http://amazing-space.stsci.edu/resources/print/activities/solsyst_tradecards_jr.pdf

32) Solar System Trading Cards – ON LINE.

Choose an object from our Solar System to name it and collect the card

http://amazing-space.stsci.edu/resources/explorations/trading/game.htm

33) Planet size comparison.

http://www.sciencenetlinks.com/interactives/messenger/psc/PlanetSize.html

2. THE EARTH AND ITS MOVEMENTS

ACTIVITIES

1) **Join with arrrows.**

Lunar Roving Vehicle

Apollo 11 - Flag

Lunar Eclipse

Footprint on the Moon

Earth from the Moon

2) The Moon.

a) The color of the Moon is ______________________

b) The Moon's surface is

rocky grassy

c) Is there air on the Moon? ______________________

3) The Earth.

a) Is Earth a rocky or gas planet? ______________

b) Is Earth the only planet in the solar system that supports life?

____

c) Is Earth hotter or colder than Mars?

____

d) What colors are Earth? ______________________________

Color it.

4) Read the text and choose the right option:

Moon: A satellite that orbits a planet. Earth has one moon. Mars has two. Some planets have no moons (Mercury and Venus). Some planets have a dozens moons (Jupiter and Saturn). Our moon orbits the Earth in about one month.

1. A moon orbits ...
   a) another moon
   b) a planet
   c) a satellite

2. Do all planets have moons?
   a) yes
   b) no
   c) sometimes

3. How many moons does Mars have?
   a) one
   b) two
   c) a dozen

4. How many moons does Jupiter have?
   a) one
   b) two
   c) a dozen

5) Remenber and complete the paragraph. Use the words in the box.

Earth	**moons**	**planets**	**rings**
Solar system	**Sun**		

The *Solar system* is very, very, big! The (1) ....is at the center. There are nine (2).............. in the Solar system. They travel round the Sun. Four of the planets have got (3)............round them. And seven planets (for example, our planet, (4).............) have got (5)................

6) Match the words to the movements.

day		**spring**
	rotation	
summer		**year**
night		**winter**
	orbit	
spin		**autumn**

7) Rotation: days and nights. Complete the sentences.

The Earth rotates on its own axis. This movement creates the difference between **day** and **night**.

The Earth takes .....hours (one day) to complete one rotation on its axis. It totates constantly without ever stopping. Rotation causes .... and....... On the half of the Earth facing the Sun, it is day. On the other half of the Earth facing away from the Sun, it is nigth. When it is night in Spain it is day in ....

8) Orbit: the seasons. Complete the sentences.

> The Earth orbits the Sun. This movement causes the different **seasons.**

The Earth takes ..... days and ....hours (one ....) to complete one orbit of the Sun. The amount of light and heat received from the Sun is not equal everywhere on Earth because the Earth spins on its .... **Its axis is tilted**, and this has an important effect.

This causes different climates in different areas of the world. It is also responsible for the changes in season during the year: **spring**, ..., ... and................

The seasons happen at different times in the two hemispheres. When it is summer in the **Northern** Hemisphere, it is winter in the .... Hemisphere.

Winter in the Northern Hemisphere

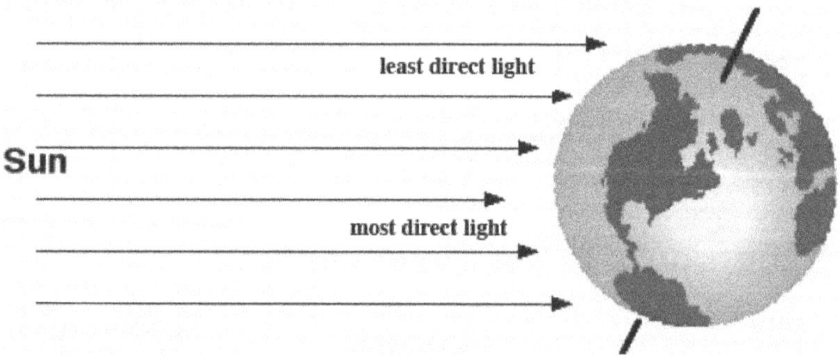

> **Axis of Rotation** - An imaginary line going from the north pole to the south pole. The earth spins on this line.

Earth's Tilt

9) Think about. ¿Summer or Winter?

10) Use the data to make a line graph.

Day	Hours of daylight
Jan. 22	9
Feb. 22	10.5
Mar. 22	12
April 22	13
May 22	14.5
June 22	16
July 22	14.5
Aug. 22	13
Sept. 22	12
Oct. 22	10.5
Nov. 22	9
Dec. 22	8 hrs

a) What season has the most hours of daylight?

b) What causes the length of daylight to change?

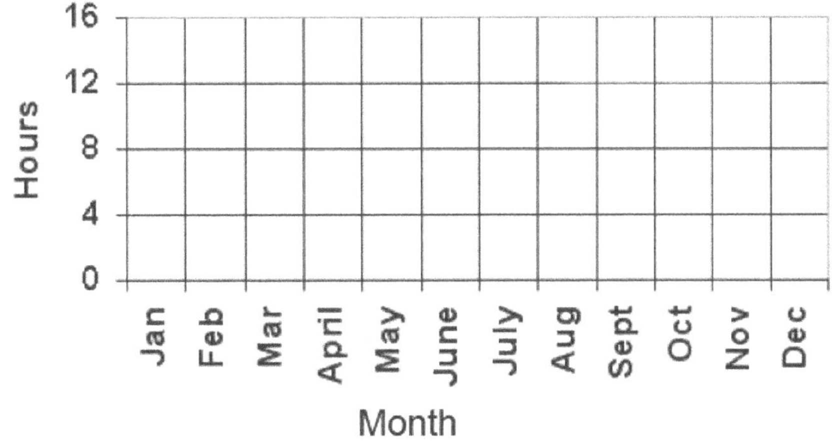

11) Lunar phases (Part One - easy). Join with arrows.

Phases of the Moon - The changes in the appearance of the moon's shape during a month.

New Moon. When the Moon is not iluminated.

Waning Moon. When the Moon is partially iluminated.

Waxing Moon. When the Moon is partially iluminated.

Half Moon. When the Moon is half iluminated.

Full Moon. When the Moon is totally iluminated.

a) Name the phases of the Moon.

b) Which phase of the Moon are we in now?

12) Lunar phases (Part two – difficult). Join with arrows.

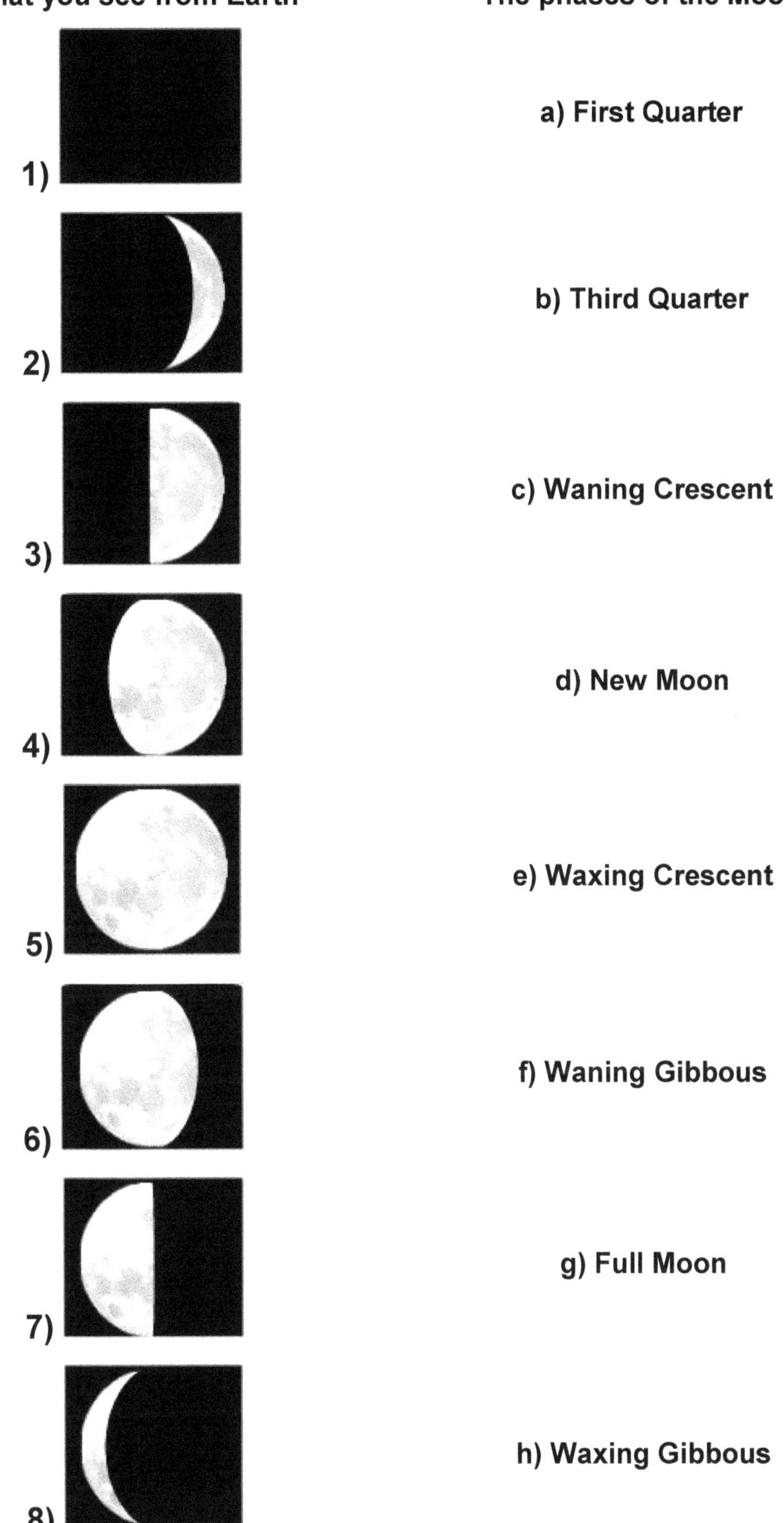

13) Lunar phases (Part Three – difficult). Join with arrows.

The Moon takes about one month (28 days) to orbit the Earth. This is called a **lunar month.**

1) days 1 and 29	**a) First Quarter**
2) 7th- 8th days	**b) Third Quarter**
3) 16th- 21st days	**c) Waning Crescent**
4) 24th- 28th	**d) New Moon**
5) 15th day	**e) Waxing Crescent**
6) 9th- 14th days	**f) Waning Gibbous**
7) 22nd- 23rd	**g) Full Moon**
8) 2nd-6th days	**h) Waxing Gibbous**

14) Label the Solar eclipse.

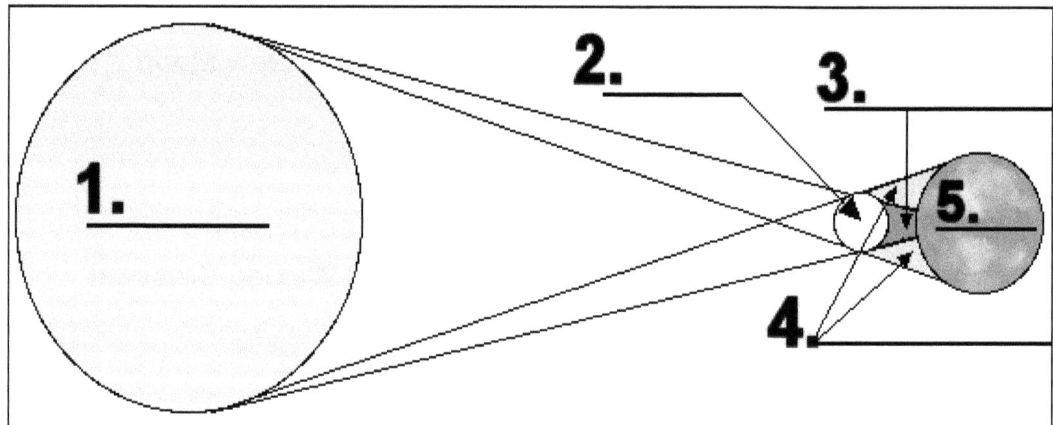

Earth: the planet on which we live.

Moon: the natural satellite of the Earth.

Penumbra: the area in which the shadow of an object (the moon on the Earth) is partial.

Sun: the star in our Solar System.

Umbra: the area in which the shadow of an object (the moon on the Earth) is total.

PENUMBRA: partial solar eclipse.
UMBRA: total solar eclipse.

15) Label the Lunar Eclipse.

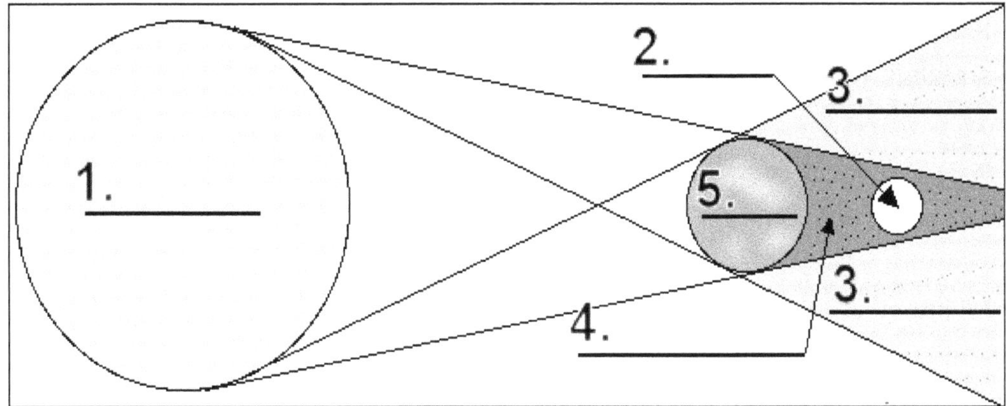

Penumbra: the area in which the shadow of an object (in this case, the Earth on the moon) is partial.

Umbra: the area in which the shadow of an object (in this case, the Earth on the moon) is total.

TOTAL LUNAR ECLIPSE: when the entire moon is in the Earth's umbra.

PARTIAL LUNAR ECLIPSE: when part of the moon is in the Earth's umbra.

16) The Earth (II).

a) The Earth is covered with ________________________.

b) The Earth is the __________ planet from the Sun.

c) The length of one day on Earth is ____ hours.

d) The Earth has ____ moon.

17) Remenber.

The biggest planet is named ....(Color ....red and yellow).

The smallest planet is named ....(Color................brown and gray).

18) Learn about the lunar phases.

http://aspire.cosmic-ray.org/

Part 1

Your job is to determine which half of the moon is receives sunlight, and which half of the Earth receives sunlight.

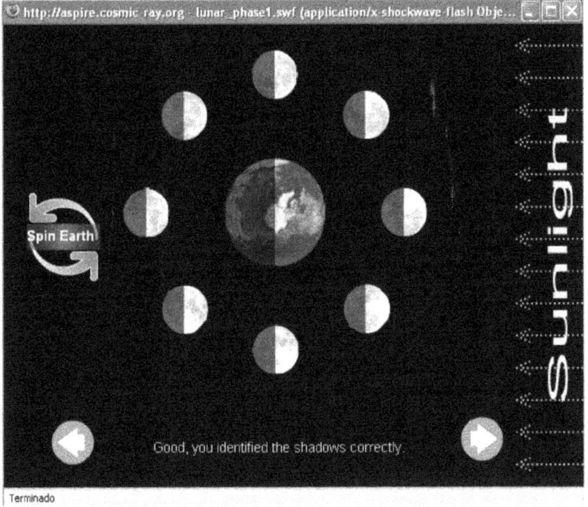

Part 2

Look at the moon when it is at position (a). It looks like half of the moon is light and half is dark. Find and click the picture that shows what the moon looks like in position (a). Your job is to continue through all the phases.

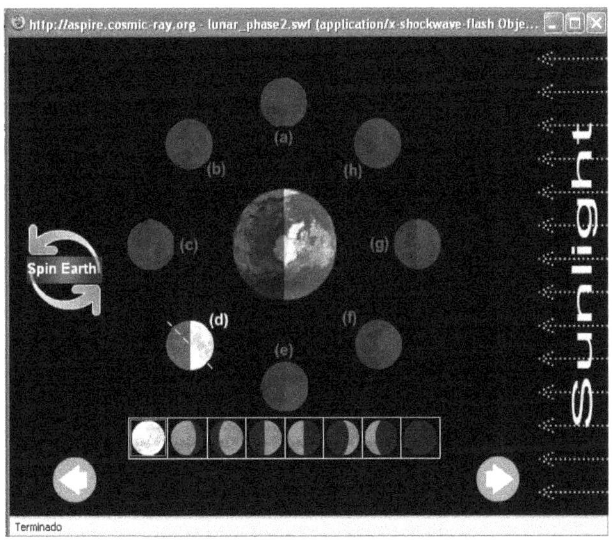

Part 3

You observe moon moving around the earth in it's orbit.

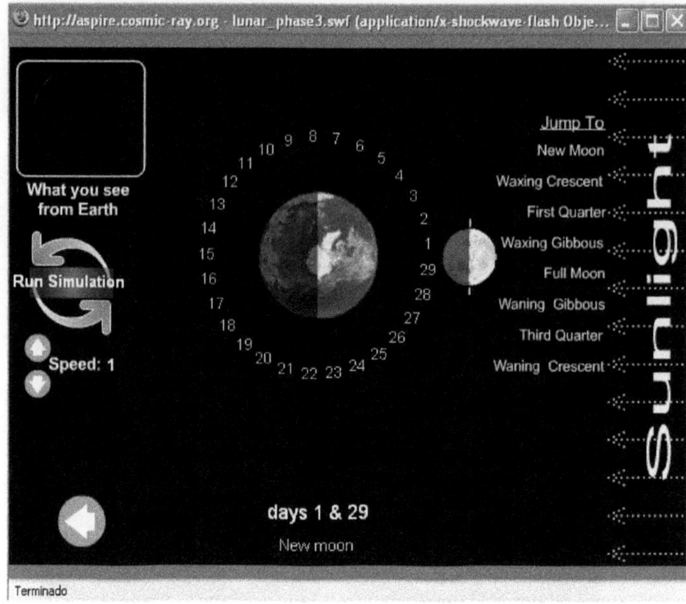

19) It's not the same. Nasa Kids' club.

http://www.nasa.gov/audience/forkids/kidsclub/flash/games/levelone/KC_Not_Same.html

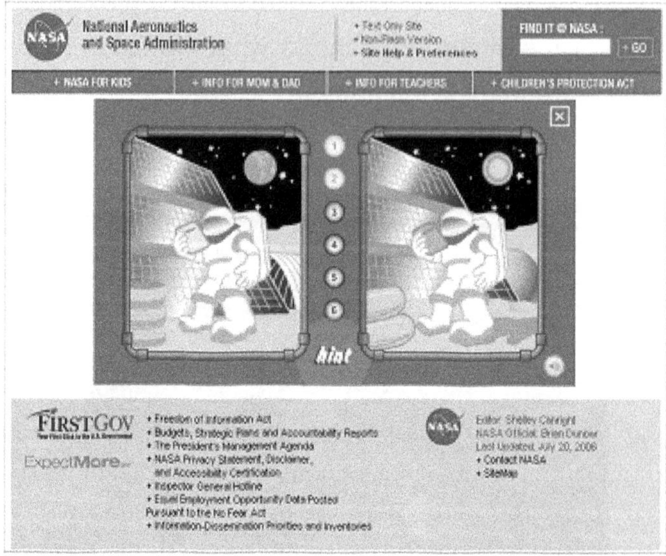

20) **Goto the head of the Solar system. Nasa Kids' club. Help to the comet get to the Sun!**

http://www.nasa.gov/audience/forkids/kidsclub/flash/games/levelfive/KC_Solar_System.html

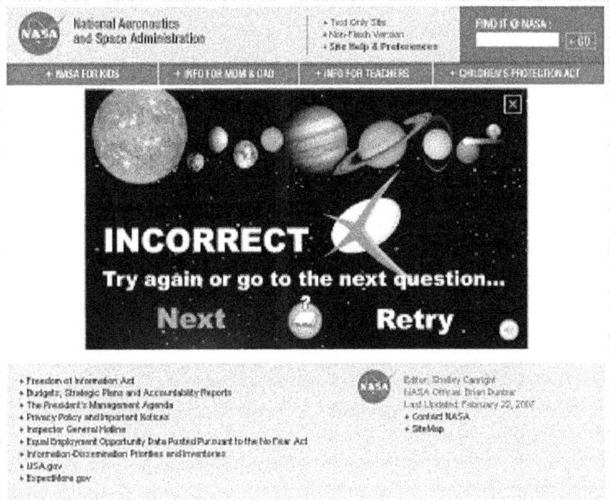

21) **Solar eclipses video.**

http://www.teachersdomain.org/resources/ess05/sci/ess/eiu/eclipse/index.html

3. PROPERTIES OF MATTER

ACTIVITIES

1) Metric System: Centimeters.

The metric system is a way to measure. Using the metric system, we use centimeters to measure how long an object is.

Use a centimeter ruler to measure the following objects:

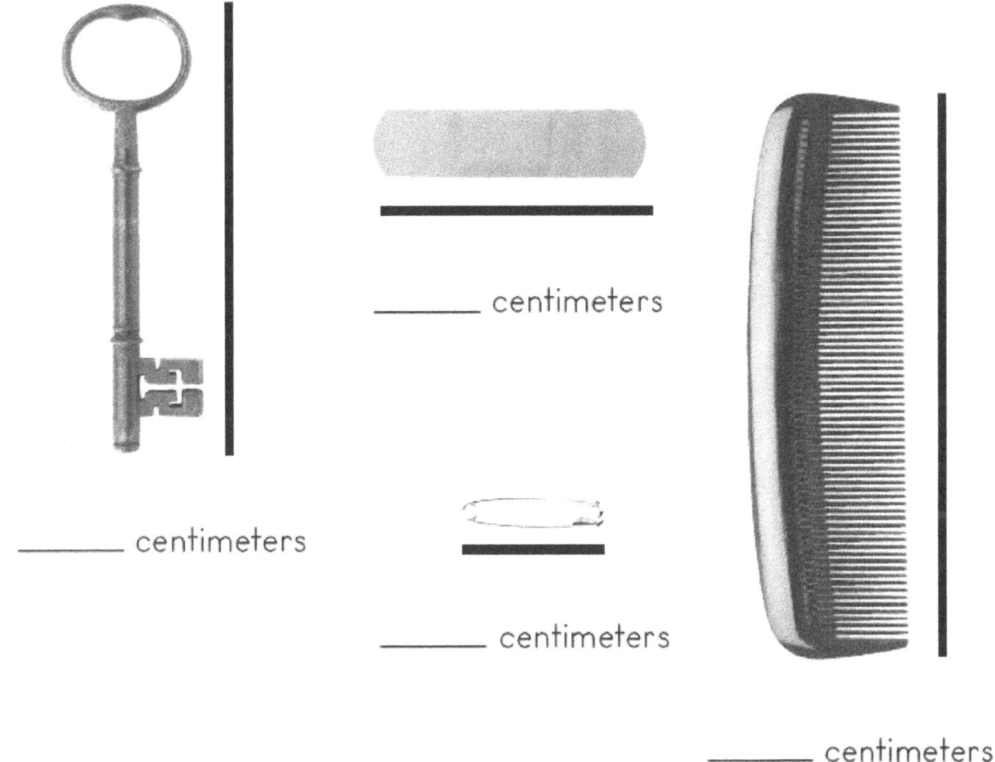

2) Centimeters.

The prefix centi- means a hundredth part. This means that 100 centimeters is the same as 1 meter.

100 centimeters = 1 meter

Use a tape measure to measure the heights of two classmates.

name

....

....................meter ....centimeters

name

....

....................meter ....centimeters

Tape measure

3) Meters and Centimeters.

Decide which unit of measurement to use for the following objects. Draw a line from the object on the left to the word on the right.

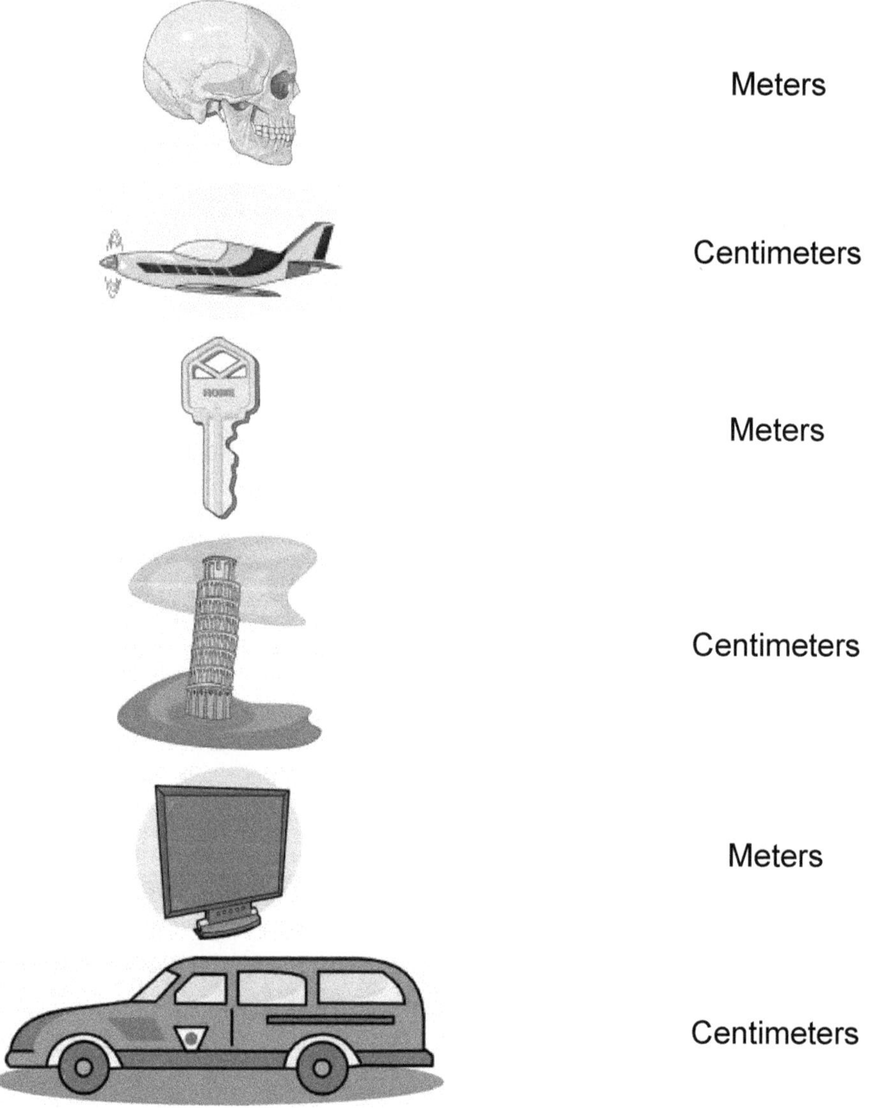

4) Height, Length, and Width.

The height of the chair is ....

The width of the chair is ....

The length of the chair is ....

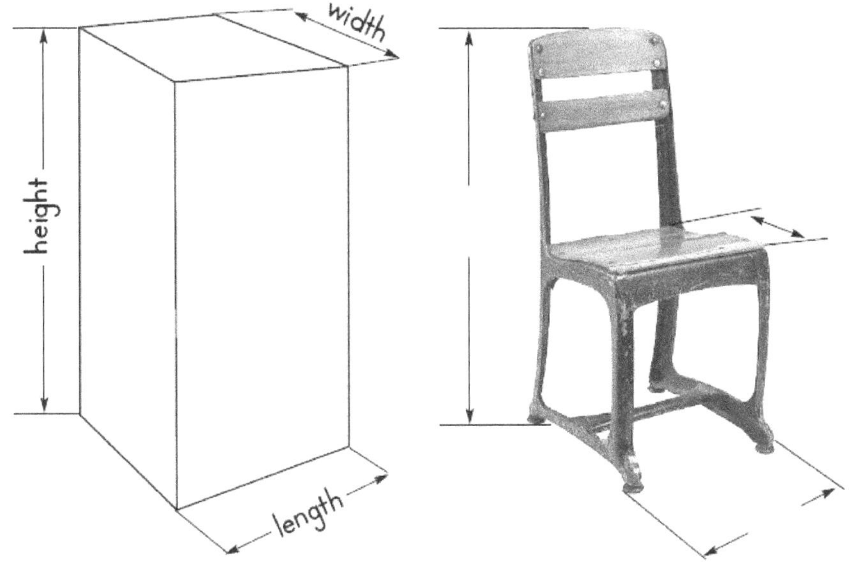

5) Conversion Practice. The ladder method.

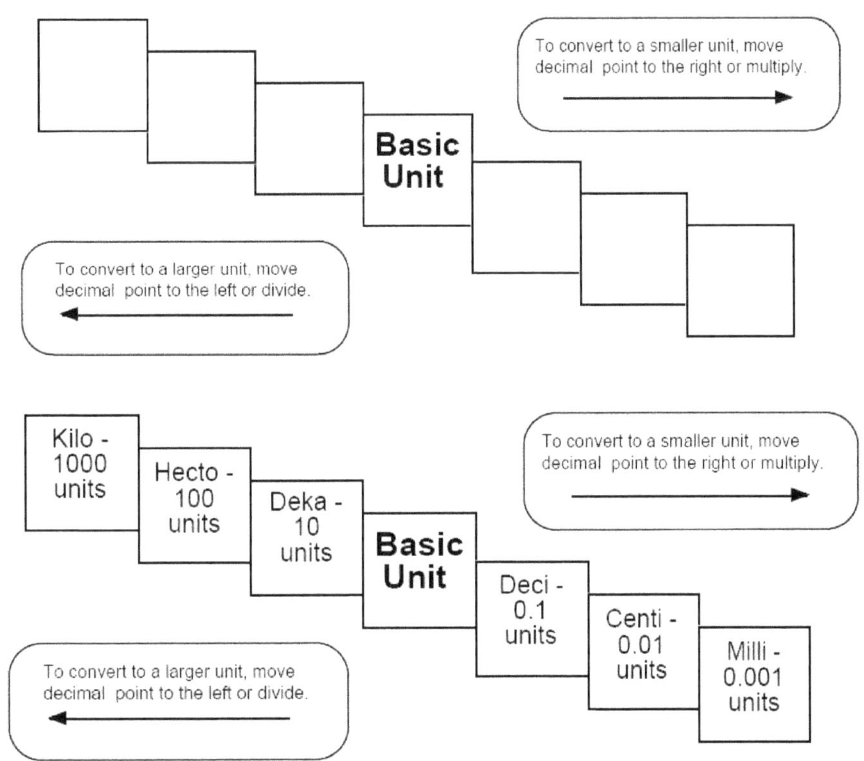

Try these conversions, using the ladder method.

1000 mg = _______ g　　　1 L = _______ mL

160 cm = _______ mm　　　14 km = _______ m

109 g = _______ kg　　　250 m = _______ km

Compare using <, >, or =.

7 g ◯ 698 mg

6) Write the correct abbreviation for each metric unit.

1) Kilogram _____
2) Meter _____
3) Gram _____
4) Milliliter _____
5) Millimeter _____
6) Liter _____
7) Kilometer _____
8) Centimeter _____
9) Milligram _____

7) Try these conversions, using the ladder method.

1) 2000 mg = _______ g
2) 104 km = _______ m
3) 480 cm = _____ m
4) 5.6 kg = _____ g
5) 8 mm = _____ cm
6) 5 L = _______ mL
7) 198 g = _______ kg
8) 75 mL = _____ L
9) 50 cm = _____ m
10) 5.6 m = _____ cm
11) 16 cm = _______ mm
12) 2500 m = _______ km
13) 65 g = _____ mg
14) 6.3 cm = _____ mm
15) 120 mg = _____ g

Compare using <, >, or =.

16) 63 cm ◯ 6 m　　17) 5 g ◯ 508 mg　　18) 1,500 mL ◯ 1.5 L

19) 536 cm ◯ 53.6 dm　　20) 43 mg ◯ 5 g　　21) 3.6 m ◯ 36 cm

8) Convert each measure to mm.

1. 92 cm 1 mm = _______ mm
2. 61 cm = _______ mm
3. 51 cm = _______ mm
4. 2 mm 735 m = _______ mm

9) Convert each measure to cm.

1. 70 mm = _______ cm
2. 73 cm 10 mm = _______ cm
3. 946 m 6 km = _______ cm
4. 317 m = _______ cm

10) Convert each measure to m.

1. 7 km = _______ m
2. 79 m 3,300 cm = _______ m
3. 12 km = _______ m
4. 9,800 cm 872 m = _______ m

11) Convert each measure to km.

1. 8,000 m = _______ km
2. 38 km 8,000 m = _______ km
3. 12,000 m = _______ km
4. 3,000 m 243 km = _______ km

12) Convert each measure to cm and m.

1. 8,389 cm 9,000 mm = _______ m _______ cm
2. 1,109 cm = _______ m _______ cm
3. 727 m 1,554 cm = _______ m _______ cm
4. 2,238 cm = _______ m _______ cm

13) Metric Weight. Convert each measure to mg.

1. 76 cg 3 mg = _______ mg
2. 83 cg = _______ mg
3. 9 cg 976 g = _______ mg
4. 32 cg = _______ mg

14) Metric Weight. Convert each measure to cg.

1. 90 mg 34 cg = _______ cg
2. 80 mg = _______ cg
3. 266 g 9 kg = _______ cg
4. 3 kg = _______ cg

15) Metric Weight. Convert each measure to g.

1. 8,000 mg = _______ g
2. 611 g 6,000 mg = _______ g
3. 696 g 8,000 mg = _______ g
4. 200 cg = _______ g

16) Metric Weight. Convert each measure to kg.

1. 3,000 g = _______ kg
2. 673 kg 9,000 g = _______ kg
3. 12,000 g = _______ kg
4. 567 kg 5,000 g = _______ kg

17) Metric Capacity. Convert each measure to mL.

1. 58 cl = _______ ml
2. 2 ml 75 cl = _______ ml
3. 21 cl = _______ ml
4. 3 ml 8 L = _______ ml

18) Metric Capacity. Convert each measure to cL.

1. 70 ml = _______ cl
2. 30 ml 6 cl = _______ cl
3. 1 kl 110 L = _______ cl
4. 80 ml = _______ cl

19) Metric Capacity. Convert each measure to L.

1. 6,100 cl 723 L = _______ L
2. 10,000 ml = _______ L
3. 10 kl = _______ L
4. 11 kl 11,000 ml = _______ L

20) Metric Capacity. Convert each measure to kL.

1. 12,000 L = _______ kl
2. 5,000 L 491 kl = _______ kl
3. 7,000 L = _______ kl
4. 2,000 L 70 kl = _______ kl

21) Join with arrows.

Mass	force of attraction between objects
Volume or Capacity	amount of matter
Weight	amount of space

22) **The Meter (Video).**

http://www.metricamerica.com/SI-Metric/meter.wmv

23) **The Kilogram (Video).**

http://www.metricamerica.com/SI-Metric/kilogram.wmv

24) **The Liter (Video).**

http://www.metricamerica.com/SI-Metric/liter.wmv

4. STATES OF MATTER

ACTIVITIES

1) Join with arrows.

Gas to Liquid	**Melting**
Liquid to Solid	**Boiling**
Solid to Gas	**Sublimating**
Liquid to Gas	**Freezing**
Solid to Liquid	**Condensing**

2) Heating and cooling.

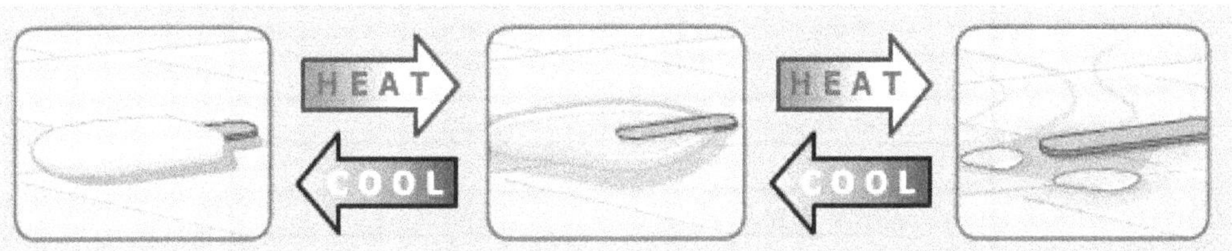

Complete the sentences with: heating, cooling, liquid, solid, gas.

a) .... a solid can turn it into a liquid.

b) Cooling a liquid can turn it into a ....

c) Heating a liquid can turn it into a ....

d) .... a liquid can turn it into a solid.

e) Cooling a gas can turn it into a ....

3) Choose the right option.

- o A: gas, B: solid, C: liquid
- o A: gas, B: liquid, C: solid
- o A:solid, B: gas, C: liquid
- o A:solid, B: gas, C: liquid

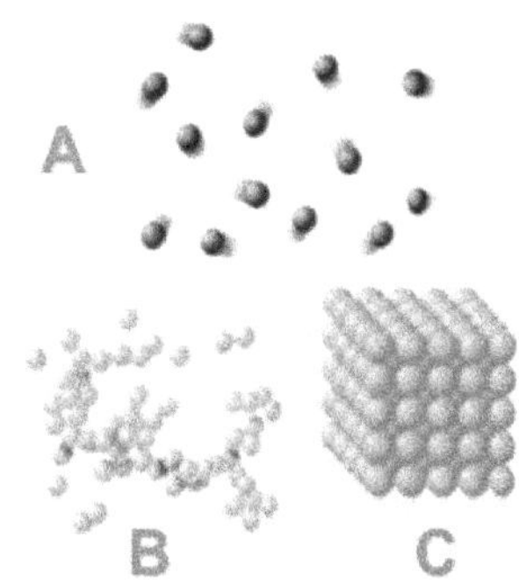

4) Melting, Boiling, Freezing and Condensing. Complete.

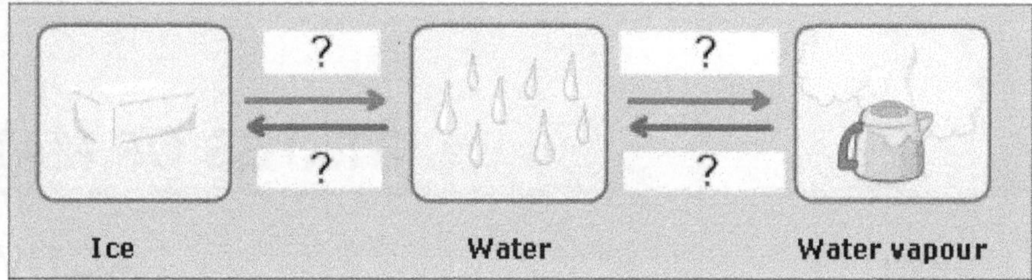

5) Solids and liquids.

Look at the table of melting point of common materials. Using the information answer the questions.

Material	Melting point (ºC)
Gold	1064
Silver	962
Iron	1525
Aluminium	660
Mercury	-39
Tin	232
Salt	800
Sugar	185
Chocolate	35
Olive oil	-20
Candle wax	60
Ice	0
Glass	1400

a) Which material has the highest melting point?

b) Which material has the lowest melting point?

c) Room temperature is 22ºC. Name three materials that are solids at room temperature?

d) Which material are liquids at room temperature?

e) Which materials have a lower melting point than ice?

f) Which material requires the most heat to melt?

6) Properties of solids, liquids an gas.

Solids	Liquids	Gases

Definite shape **Definite volume** **No definite shape** **No definite volume**	**Can flow** **Cannot flow**	**Can be compressed** **Cannot be compressed**

7) Phases of matter. Complete.

Gas

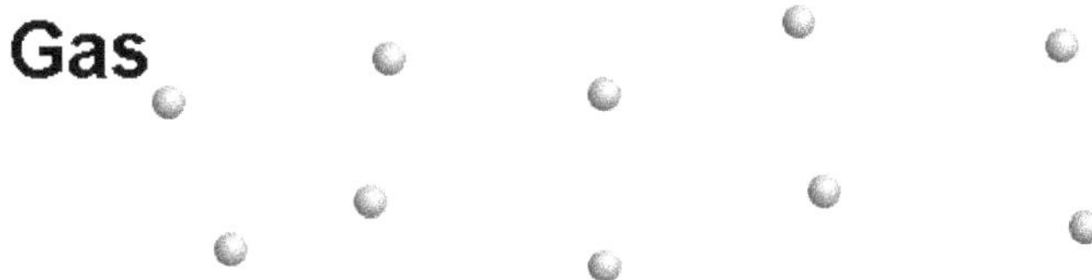

The gaseous phase of water is called ....

Another example of gas is ....

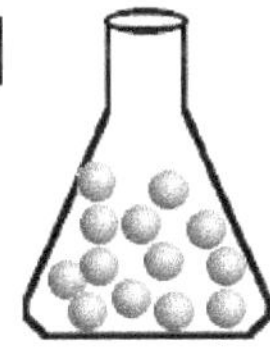

The liquid phase of water is called ....

Another example of liquid is ....

Solid

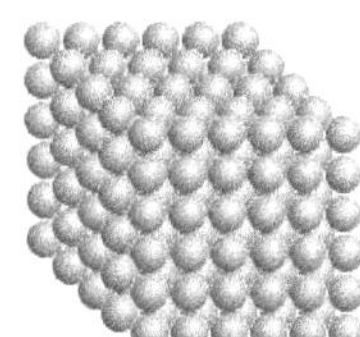

The solid phase of water is called ....

Another example of solid is ....

8) Choose the right option.

a) When a liquid is cooled, it turns into a solid. This is called ...

- dissolving
- Freezing
- Melting

b) Evaporation is when

- a gas is cooled and changes to a liquid
- a liquid is heated and changes to a gas
- a solid is heated and changes to a liquid

c) Condensation happens when

- a gas is cooled
- a liquid is cooled
- a solid is cooled

d) When a solid is heated, it turns into a liquid. This is called ...

- dissolving
- freezing
- melting

e) Which of the following are examples of liquids?

- Wood and paper
- Shampoo and oil
- Shoes and socks

f) A gas condenses into a liquid when it is...

- Cooled
- Warmed
- Boiled

9) Changing state. Can you turn the ice to water?

http://www.bbc.co.uk/schools/ks2bitesize/science/activities/changing_state.shtml

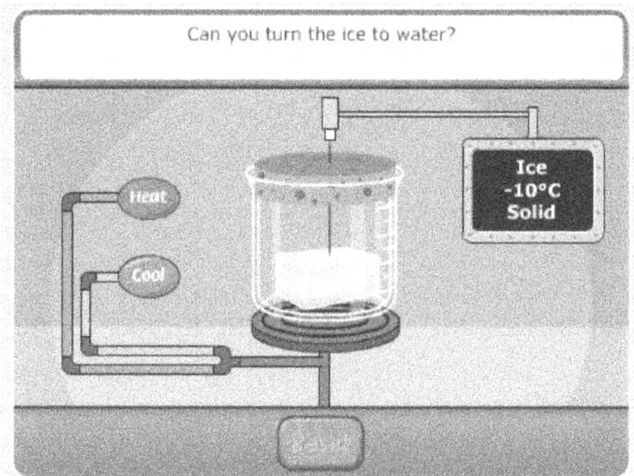

10) Solid and liquid: melting point.

http://www.bbc.co.uk/schools/ks2bitesize/science/activities/solids_liquids.shtml

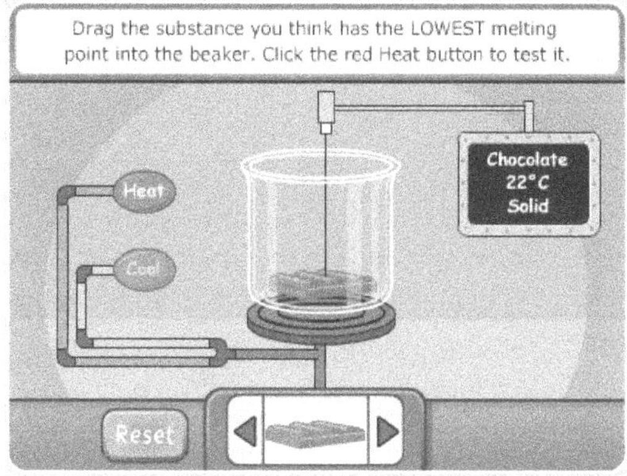

11) Three states of matter in action.

http://www.harcourtschool.com/activity/states_of_matter/index.html

5. PURE AND MIXED SUBSTANCES

ACTIVITIES

1) What do you remenber? solid, liquid or gas.

Solid, liquid and gas are called the three states of matter. The particles in a solid, liquid are shown bellow. The arrows represent changes of states:

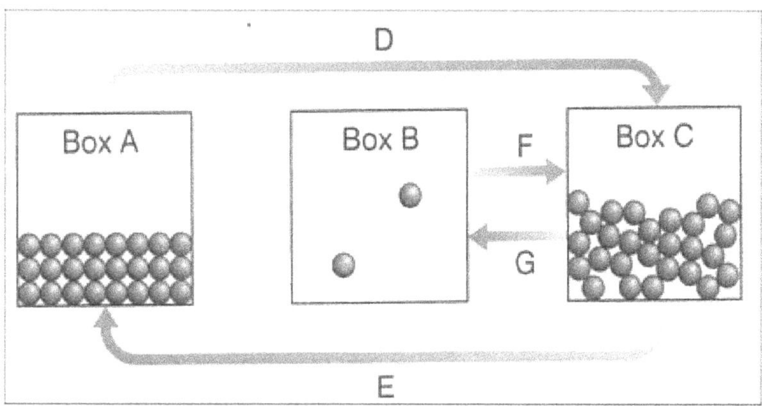

a) Which box contains:

a solid?

a liquid?

a gas?

b) Which state of matter is most easily compressed?

c) Identify the cahnges of state labelled D, E, F annd G.

D is called...............

E is called...............

F is called...............

G is called...............

d) Which changes of state require cooling to take place?

.... and ....

2) Join with arrows.

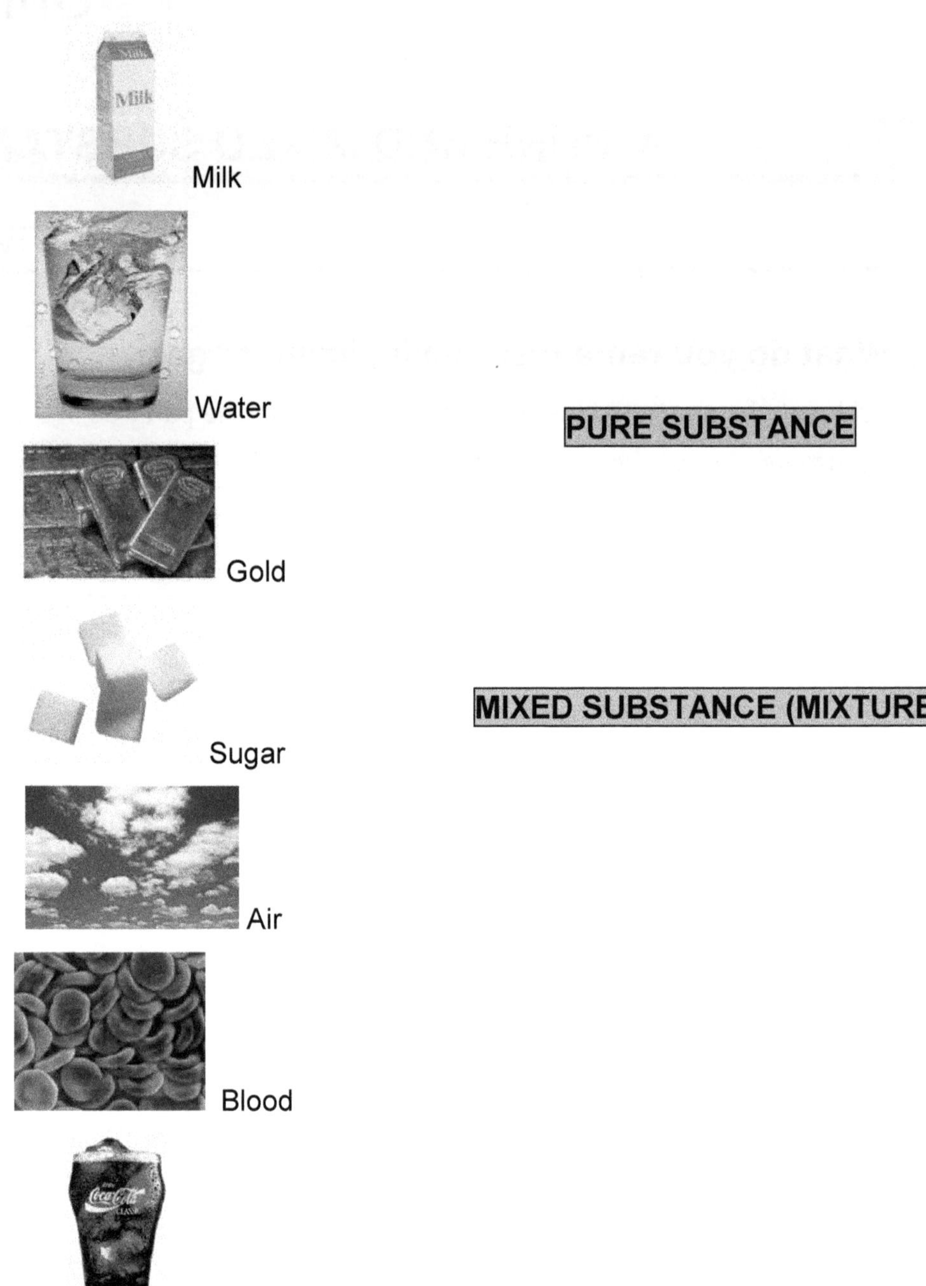

3) Separating mixtures. Complete the sentences.

Use the words in the box.

Chromatography	**Filtration**	**Evaporation**	**Distillation**

.... is good for separating a liquid from a solution.

.... is good for separating dissolved substances that have different colours

.... is good for separating a soluble solid from a liquid.

.... is good for separating an insoluble solid from a liquid.

4) Use words from the box to label the diagrams.

solute solution solvent suspension sediment

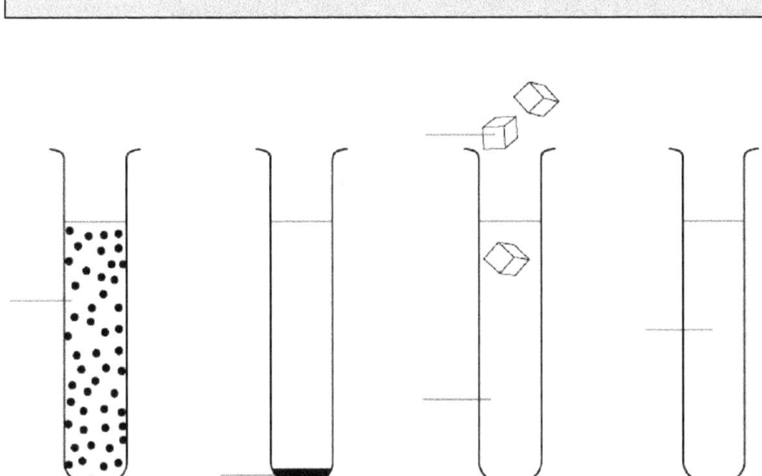

5) Each verb in the table represents a separation process. Write down the corresponding noun.

Verb	evaporate	distil	filter	crystallise
Noun				

6) Experiment: Separating a sand and salt mixture.

In this experiment simple processes are used to separate salt from a sand and salt mixture.

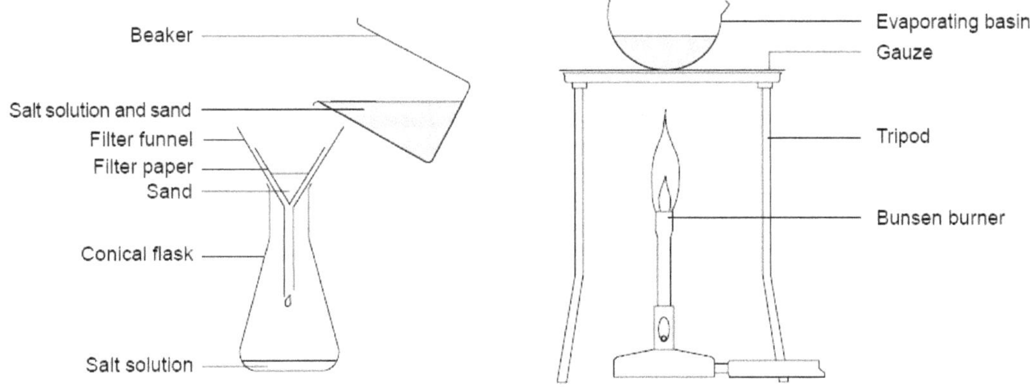

1. Mix about 5 g of the mixture with 50 cm^3 of water in a 250 cm^3 beaker. Stir gently.
2. Filter the mixture into a conical flask and pour the filtrate into an evaporating basin.
3. Heat the salt solution gently until it starts to 'spit'.
4. Turn off the Bunsen burner.

Safety: wear eye protection.

To spit: chisporrotear

7) For each diagram, use words from the box to:

a) label the equipment
b) write the method of separation under the diagram.

beaker	evaporation
Bunsen burner	filtration
conical flask	filter funnel
crystal	filter paper
crystallisation	sediment
decanting	sieve
delivery tube	sieving
distillation	test-tube
evaporating dish	

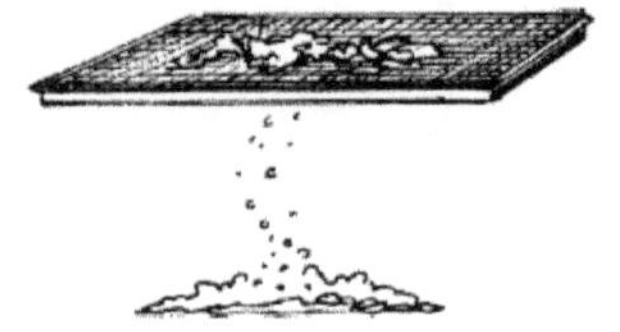
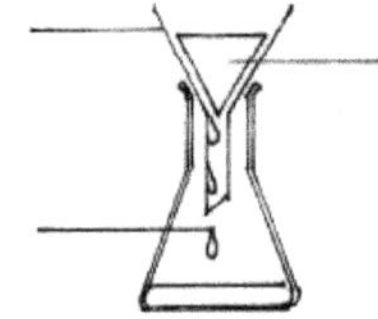
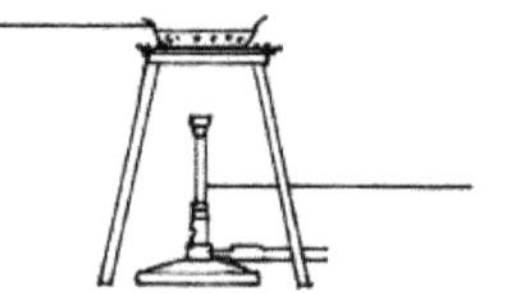

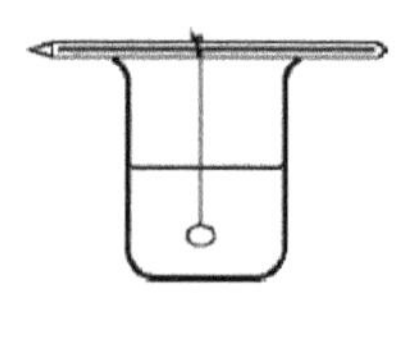
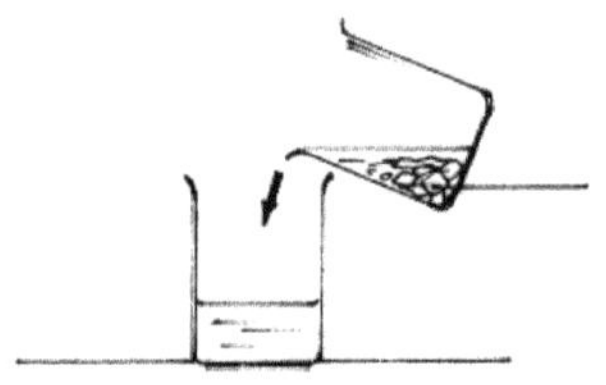
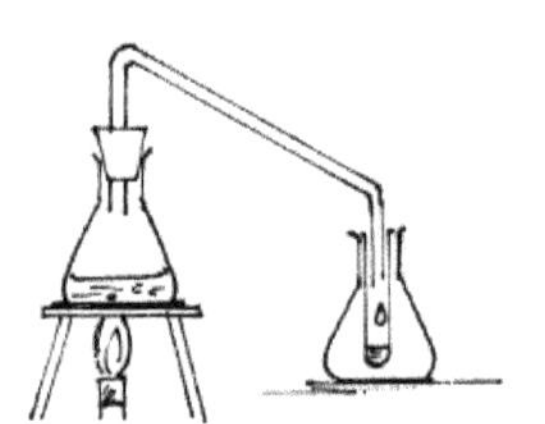

8) Experiment: Extracting Iron from breakfast cereal.

Magnetism is good for separating magnetic solids from nonmagnetic solids.

Many breakfast cereals are fortified with iron (such as Total, Special K, etc...).

What do I need?

- breakfast cereal fortified with iron (cornflakes work, but check on the side of the packet to see what the iron content is – the higher, the better)
- a plastic cup
- a spoon
- a blender
- hot water
- a very strong magnet

Procedure

- Place approximately one cup water and one cup of cereal in the blender, let sit for a few minutes until the cereal is soft.
- Hold the magnet to the outside of the blender while it is whirling. Stop the blender.

Join with arrows.

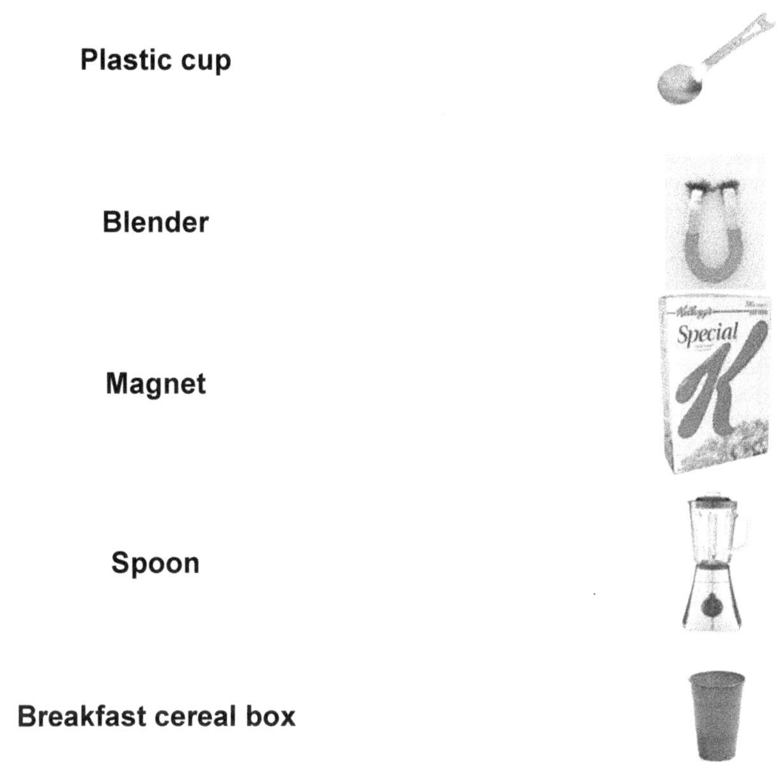

Plastic cup

Blender

Magnet

Spoon

Breakfast cereal box

Draw the experiment in three step:

1)	2)	3)

9) Experiment: Distilling mixtures.

Distillation is the separation of a liquid from a solution by boiling and condensing.

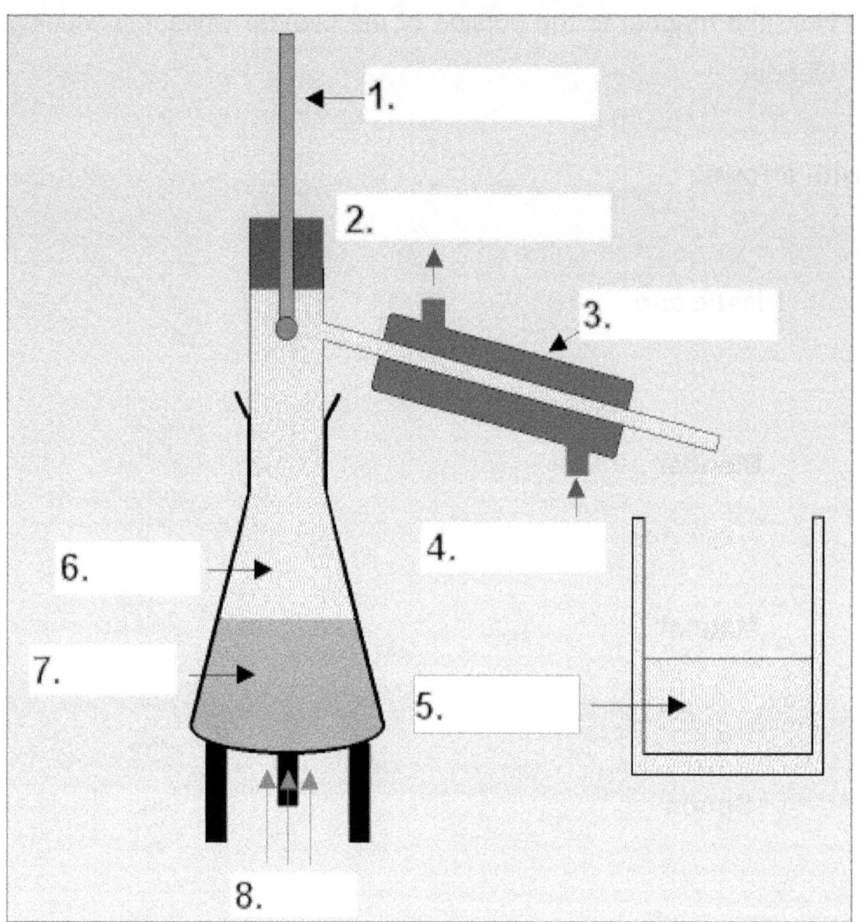

Use words from the box to label the diagram:

Thermometer	Cold water out
Vapour	Distillate
Solution	Heat
Cold water in	Condenser

a) What would be the temperature on the thermometer?

b) What is the function of **3.**?

c) What do we call this process?

10) What happens when solids dissolve in liquids (Explaining how solids dissolve). Sugar and water (Coloring particles).

The diagrams represent the particles present at the different stages when sugar is dissolved in water.

Coloring instructions

Sugar and sugar particles: red.

Water and water particles: cyan.

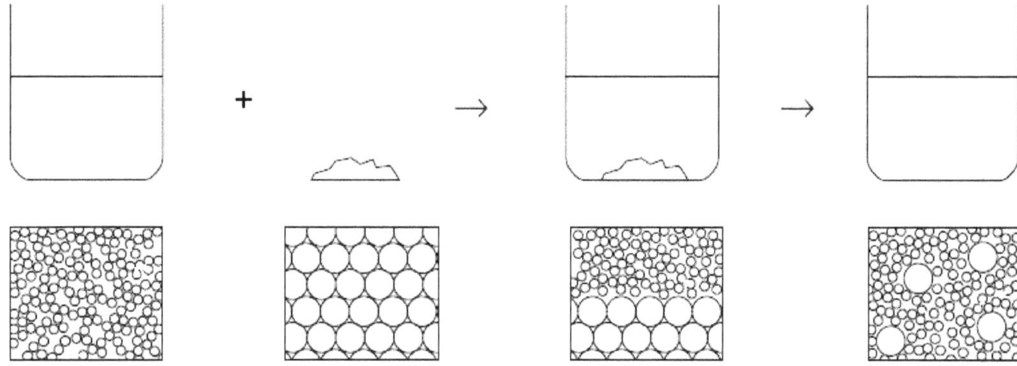

Use words from the box to label the diagram:

Solute particles	Solvent particles	Dissolving

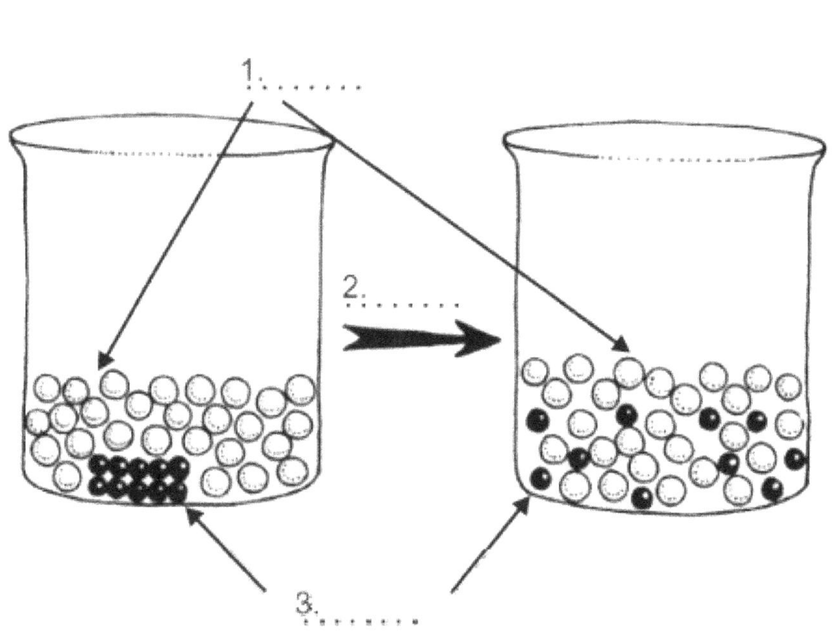

11) Filtering.

http://www.bbc.co.uk/schools/ks3bitesize/flash/7562.swf

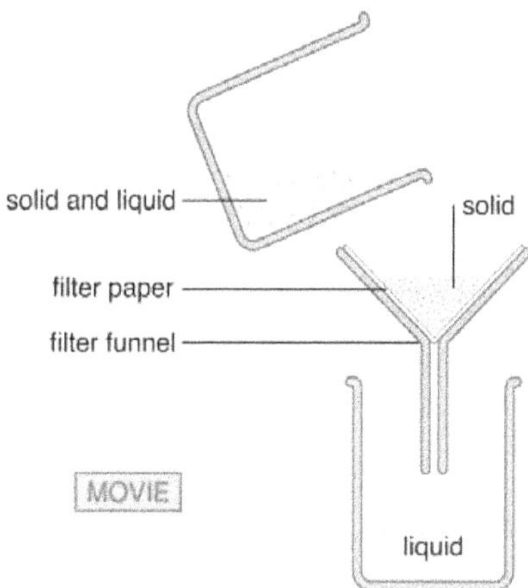

12) Distillation.

http://www.bbc.co.uk/schools/ks3bitesize/flash/7564.swf

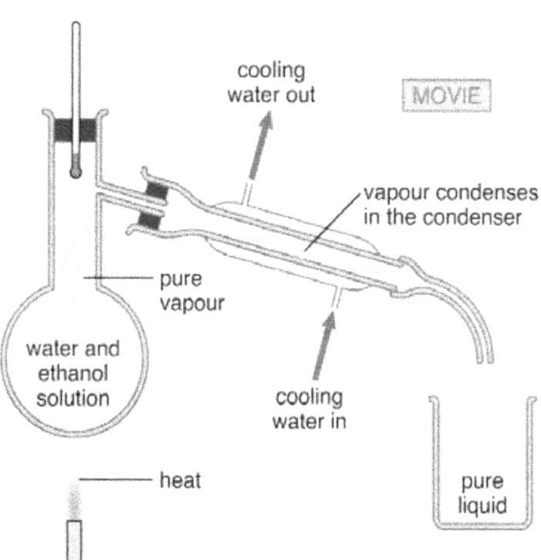

6. ELEMENTS, COMPOUNDS OR MIXTURES?

ACTIVITIES

1) **What do you remenber? Separating componets of a heterogeneous mixtures. Join with arrows.**

by magnetism	sand and water
by filtration	oil and water
by decanting	sand and iron particles

2) **Classify each of the pictures. Each circle represents an atom and each different color (black and white) represents a different kind of atom. If two atoms are touching then they are bonded together.**

A= Element
B= Compound
C= Mixture of elements
D= Mixture of compounds
E= Mixture of elements and compounds

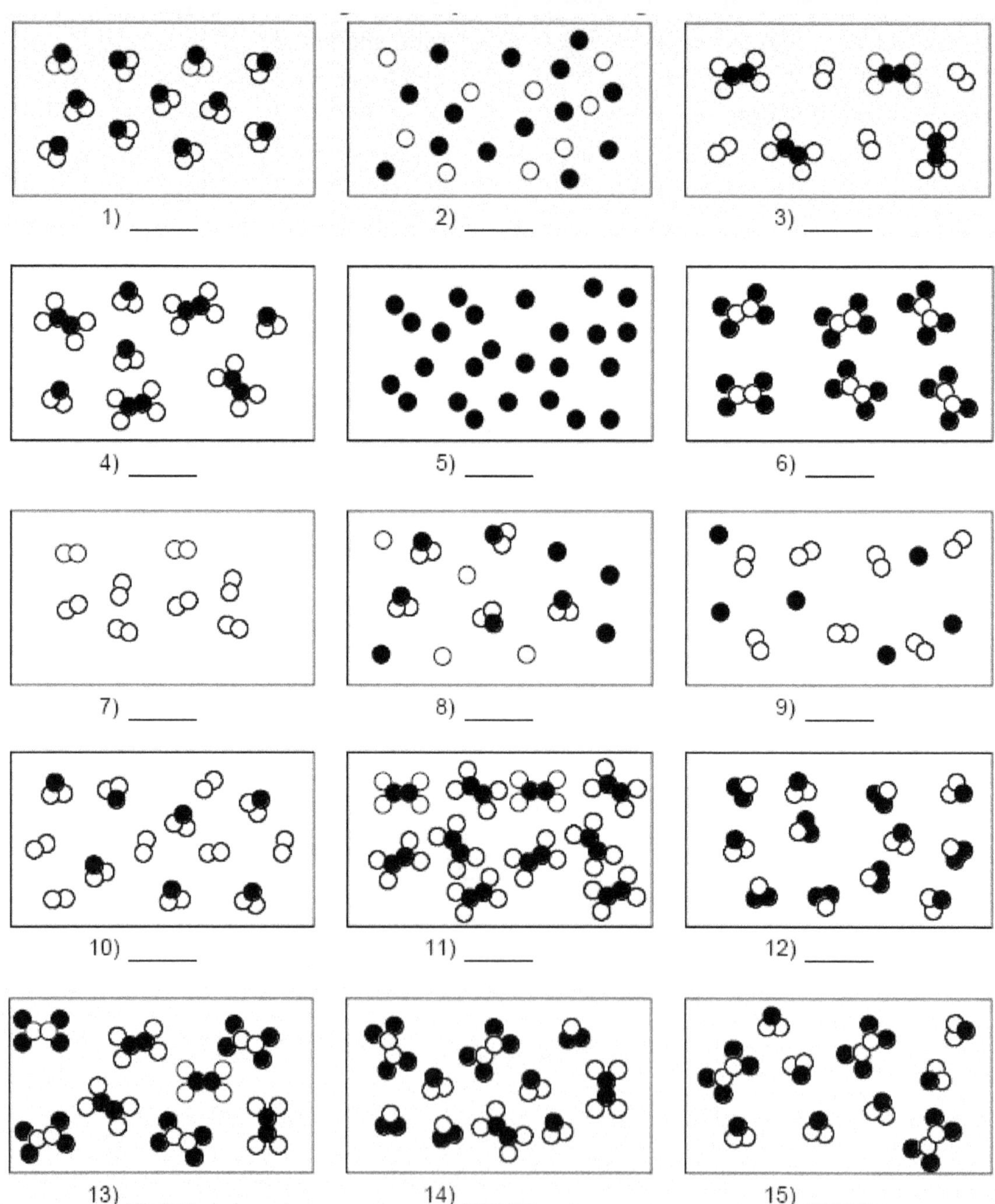

3) Link (Join with arrows) each diagram with its description.

Coloring instructions: Y= yellow, G= green, B= blue.

Diagram

a) 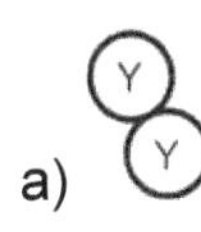

b) G

Description

1) Atom

A single particle

2) Molecule

1 particle made of 2 or more atoms

Diagram

a) 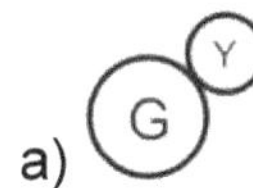

b) 

c) 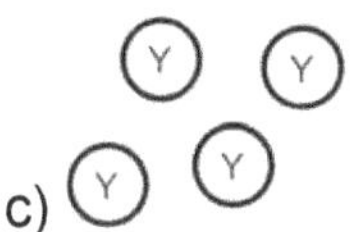

Description

1) Element

A collection of atoms that are all the same

2) Molecule

Two or more different elements joinned together

3) Mixture

Different substances mixed together but not joined

4) Study the diagrams, and decide which one each statement bellow is describing.

- Atoms of an element .....
- Molecules of an element .....
- A mixture of 2 elements, both of which are made of atoms .....
- A pure compound made of molecules .....

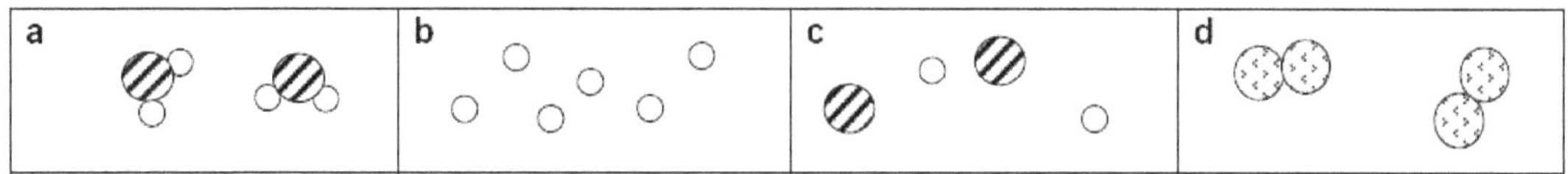

5) Made up off...

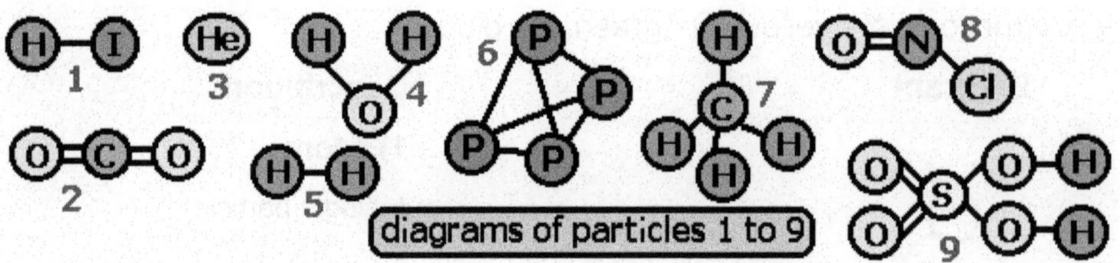

a) Which particle is a **compound made up of two elements**?

b) Which particle is a **compound made up of three elements**?

6) In the particle diagram, which substances are elements and whih substances are compounds?

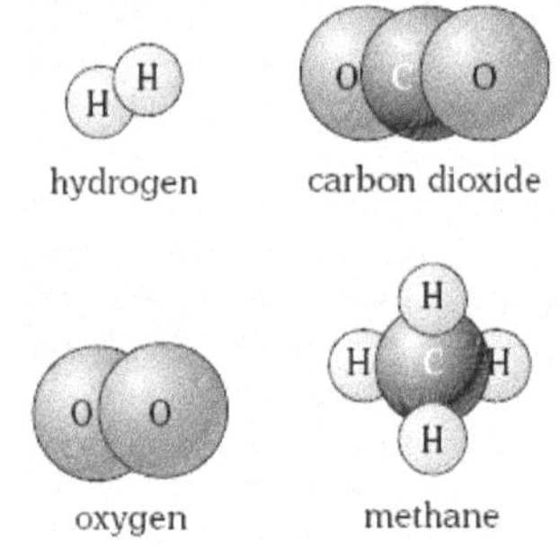

7) Which particle diagram represents a sample containing the compound CO(gas)?

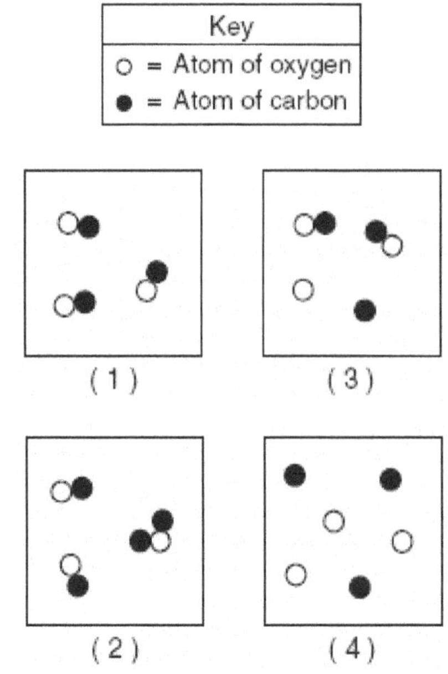

8) **On the following pictures you will find six diagrams showing the particles in some samples of materials.**

The different particles are shown as:

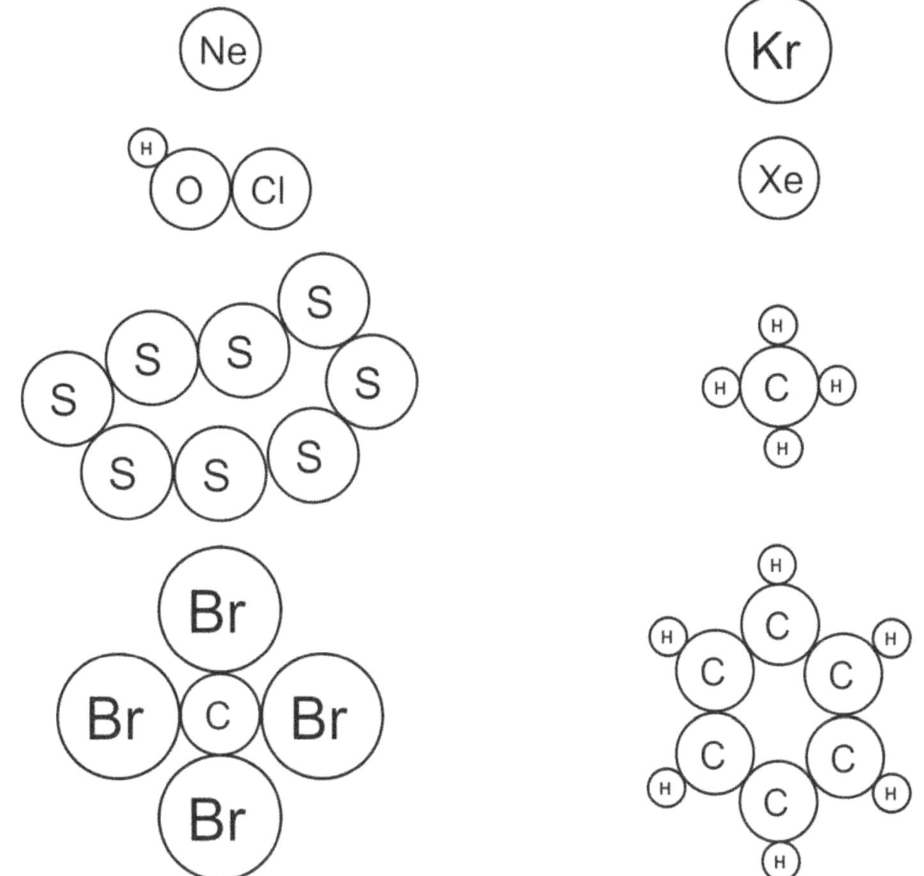

Atoms coloring instructions

Ne (orange)	O (blue)
Kr (pink)	H (red)
Xe (white)	Br (purple)
Cl (green)	C (grey)
S (yellow)	

Decide whether each diagram represents an element, a compound, or a mixture.

Diagram 1

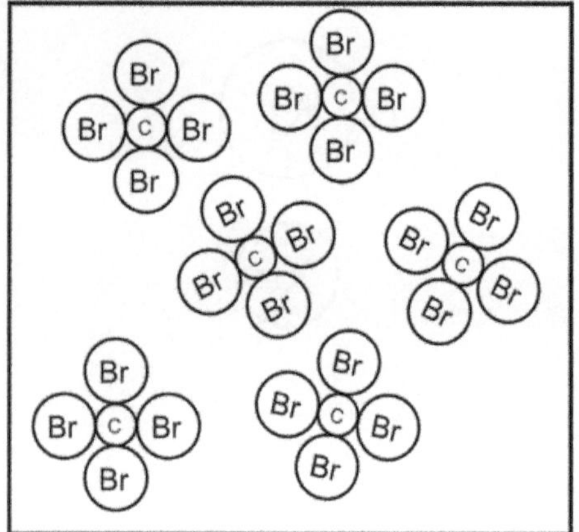

This diagram shows particles in ....

Diagram 2

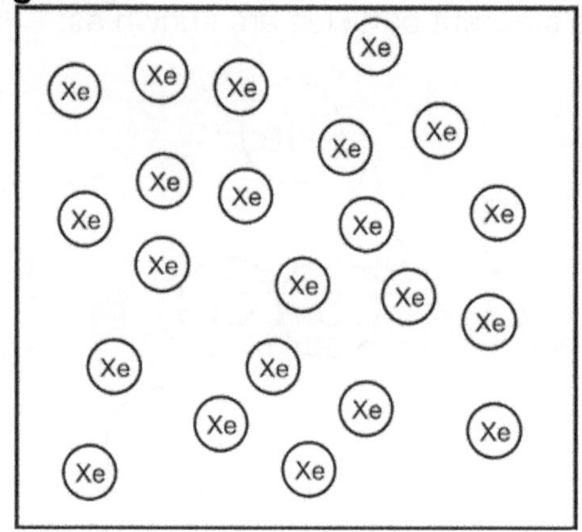

This diagram shows particles in ....

Diagram 3

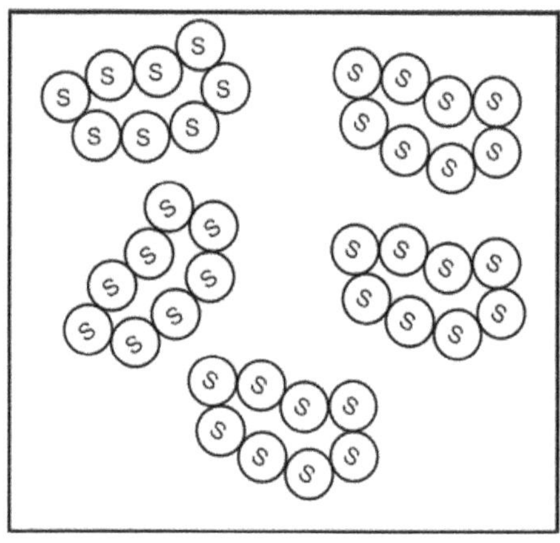

This diagram shows particles in ....

Diagram 4

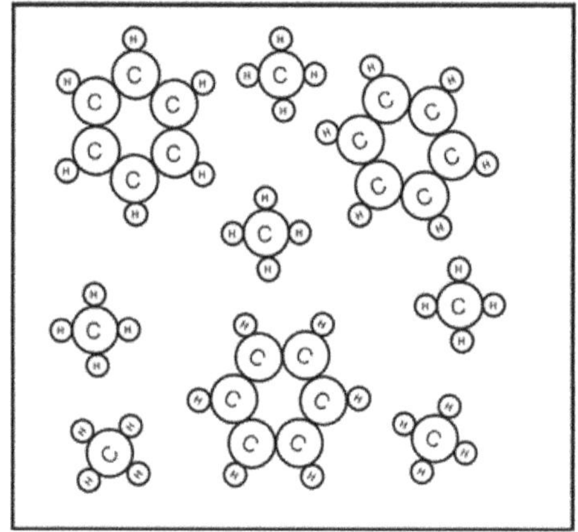

This diagram shows particles in ....

Diagram 5

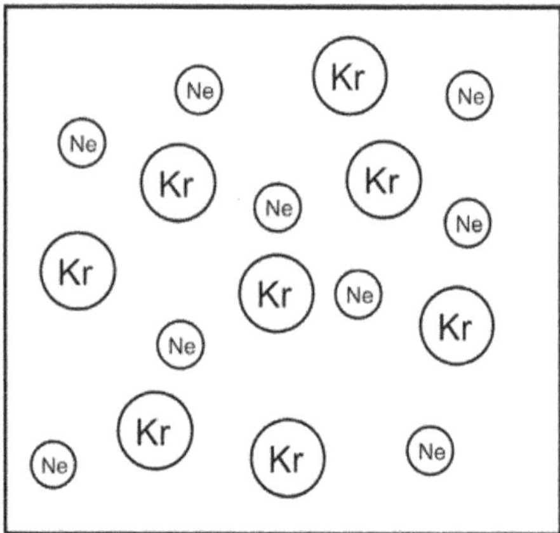

This diagram shows particles in ....

Diagram 6

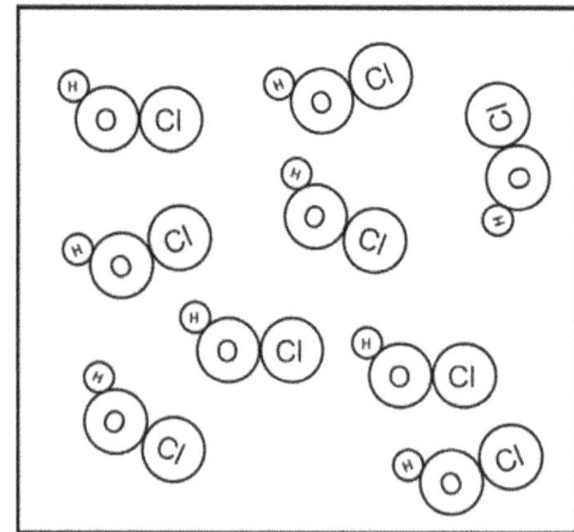

This diagram shows particles in ....

9) Different substances contain different molecules.

The three diagrams show two different substances. Which two diagrams show the same substance?

Coloring instructions: N= orange, O= blue.

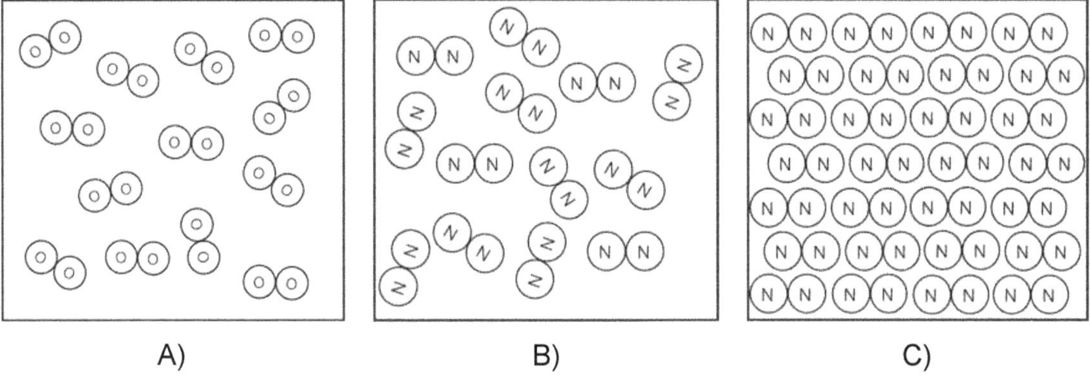

A) B) C)

10) A mixture contains more than one type of atom or molecule. Single substance or mixture?

Look at the diagrams and label each of them as either a **single substance**, or a **mixture.**
Coloring instructions: C= grey, H= red.

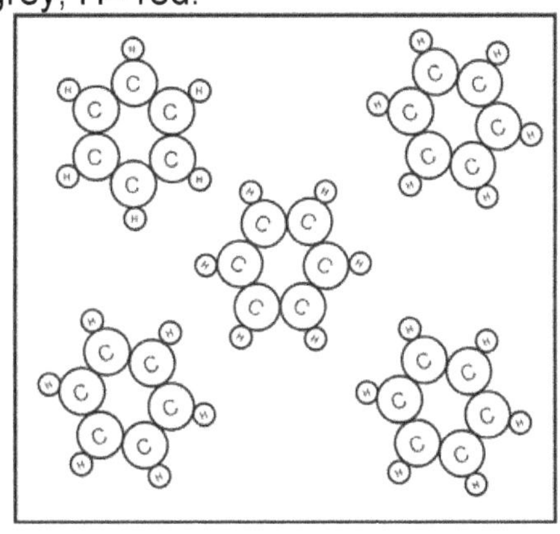

1)......................

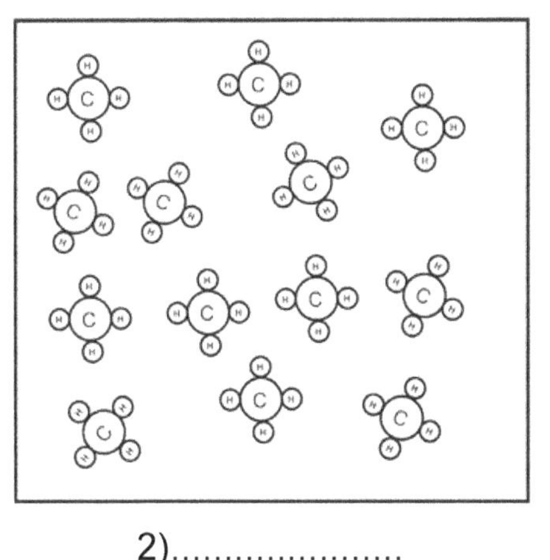

2)......................

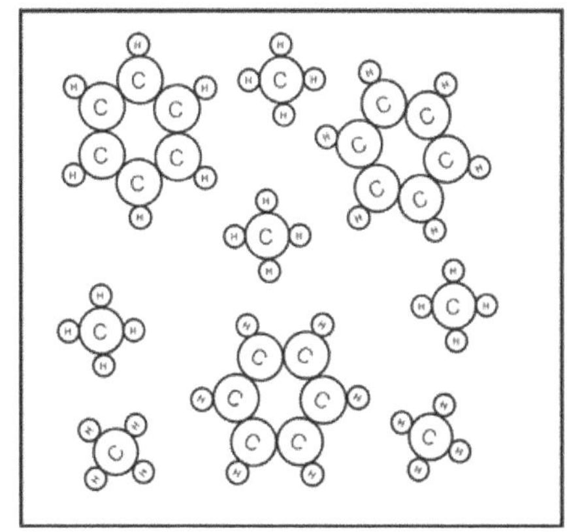

3)......................

11) Complete the sentences. Single substance or mixture?

The following two diagrams show a single substance and a mixture.

Coloring instructions: S= yellow, O= blue, H= red, C= gray.

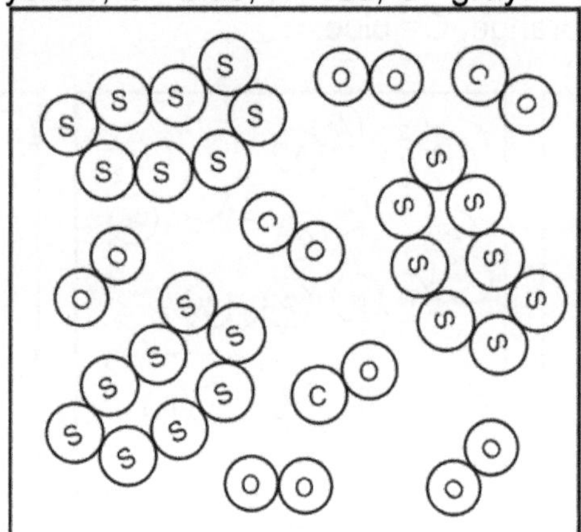

This diagram shows a ....because there is more than one type of ....

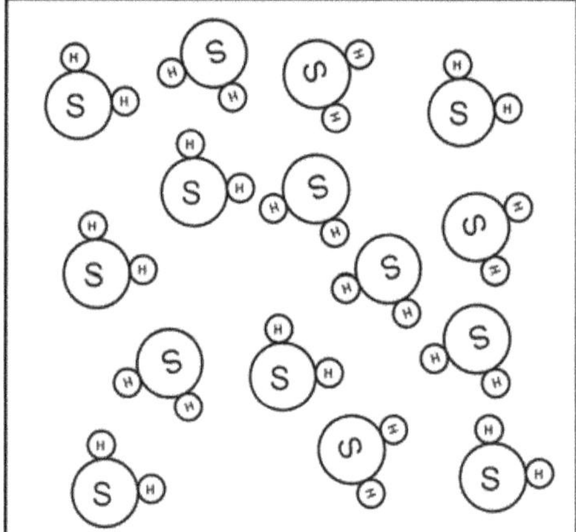

This diagram shows a ....because there is more than one type of ....

12) Complete the sentences. Molecule of an element and a molecule of a compound.

The following two diagrams show a **molecule of an element** and a **molecule of a compound.**

Coloring instructions: N= orange, H= red, P= purple.

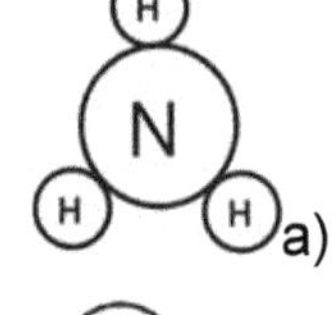

a) This diagram shows ....
because there is more than one type of ....

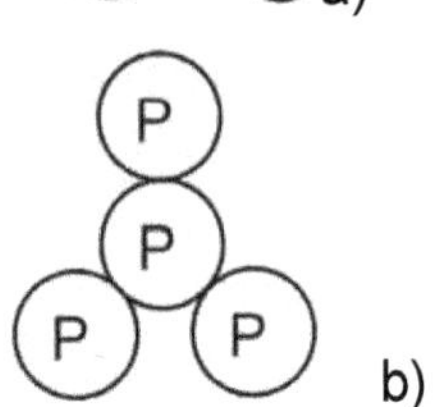

b) This diagram shows ....
because there is more than one type of ....

13) Complete the labels. Mixture, element and compound.

Coloring instructions: N= orange, H= red, Cl= green, Br= purple.

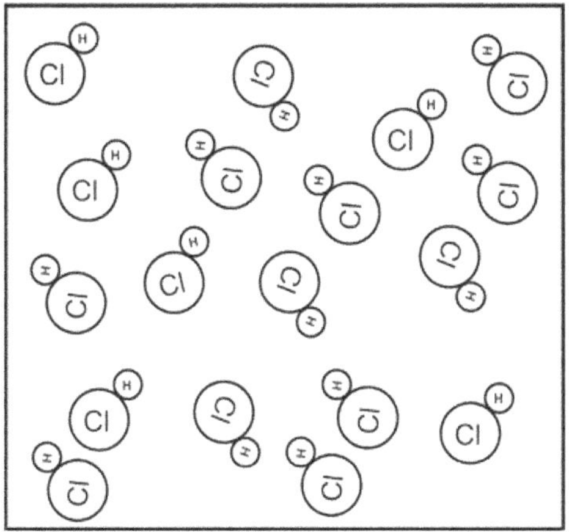

1) ....

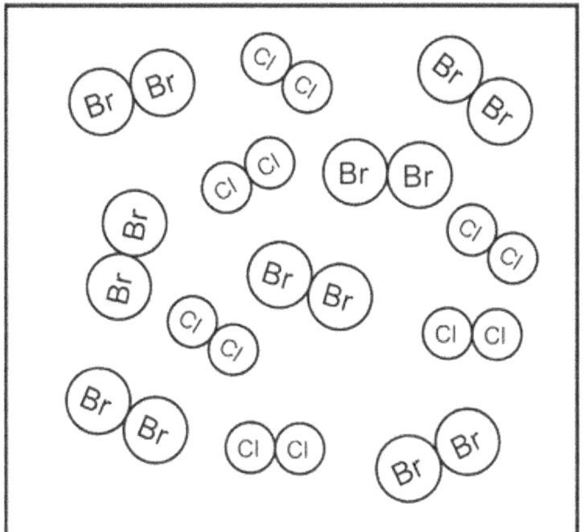

2) ....

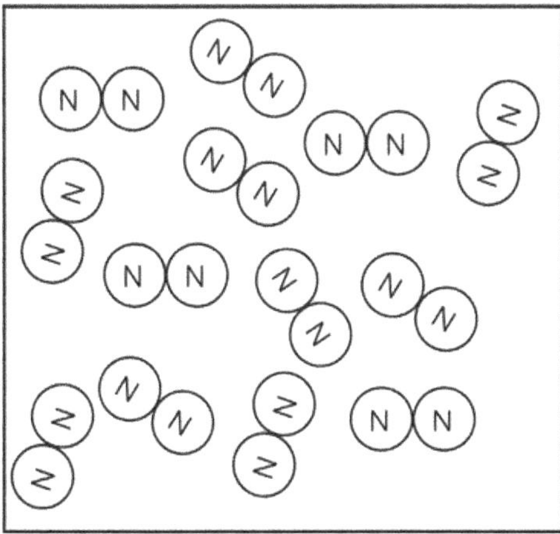

3) ....

14) Elements, Mixtures and Compounds. Online quiz.

http://www.darvill.clara.net/hotpots/emc.htm

Elements, Mixtures and Compounds

Here are pictures of some different particle arrangements. Choose the correct letters in the boxes on the right.

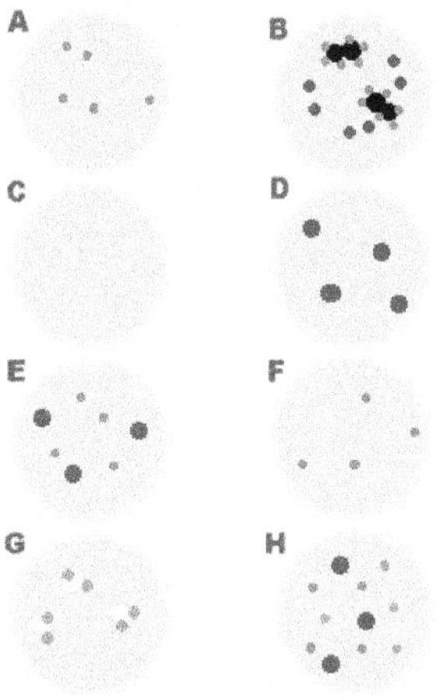

A B C D E F G H

Pure elements	CHOOSE	
Elements made of SINGLE ATOMS	CHOOSE	
An element made of MOLECULES	CHOOSE	
Mixture of TWO elements	CHOOSE	
Mixture of THREE elements	CHOOSE	
Pure compounds	CHOOSE	
Mixture of TWO compounds	CHOOSE	

Your score is: Check

Go back to previous page

VOCABULARY AND NOTES

www.ingramcontent.com/pod-product-compliance
Ingram Content Group UK Ltd.
Pitfield, Milton Keynes, MK11 3LW, UK
UKHW050614260726
13967UKWH00008B/2857